Magical Kingdom

THE ULTIMATE COLORING EXPERIENCE

Roger Burrows

To my daughter, Katy.

Printed in China

Books published by Running Press are available at special discounts for bulk purchases in the United States by corporations, institutions, and other organizations. For more information, please contact the Special Markets Department at the Perseus Books Group, 2300 Chestnut Street, Suite 200, Philadelphia, PA 19103, or call (800) 810-4145, ext. 5000, or e-mail special.markets@perseusbooks.com.

9   8   7   6   5   4   3   2   1
Digit on the right indicates the number of this printing

Library of Congress Control Number: 2009943429

ISBN 978-0-7624-3974-4

Cover design by Ryan Hayes
Edited by Lisa Cheng
Typography: Verlag

Published by Running Press Kids
an imprint of Running Press Book Publishers
A Member of the Perseus Books Group
2300 Chestnut Street
Philadelphia, PA 19103-4371

Visit us on the web!
www.runningpress.com

Hidden IMAGES

Magical Kingdom

THE ULTIMATE COLORING EXPERIENCE

Roger Burrows

RP | KIDS

PHILADELPHIA • LONDON

INTRODUCTION

The designs in this book were created to stimulate the visual imagination. When you look at each design, relax your vision and search for large and small images, complete scenes, or abstract patterns. Any shape that you find can be found again and again in the same direction, but also rotated and reflected. Designs are repeated so you can explore images in different ways, but the images are only intended as starting points. Use the visual examples given to discover castles, princesses, dragons, and the things that you might find in a magical kingdom, but use your imagination to find images and patterns of your own.

Use felt pens, colored pencils, markers, pastels, or even paints to color within the lines or across them. You can even choose to enlarge the designs onto fabric, wood, or canvas. You may want to frame some of the designs, or use them for greeting cards, decorations, and presents. The possibilities are limitless. Please visit my website at www.rogerburrowsimages.com.

Hope you enjoy this book!

— Roger Burrows

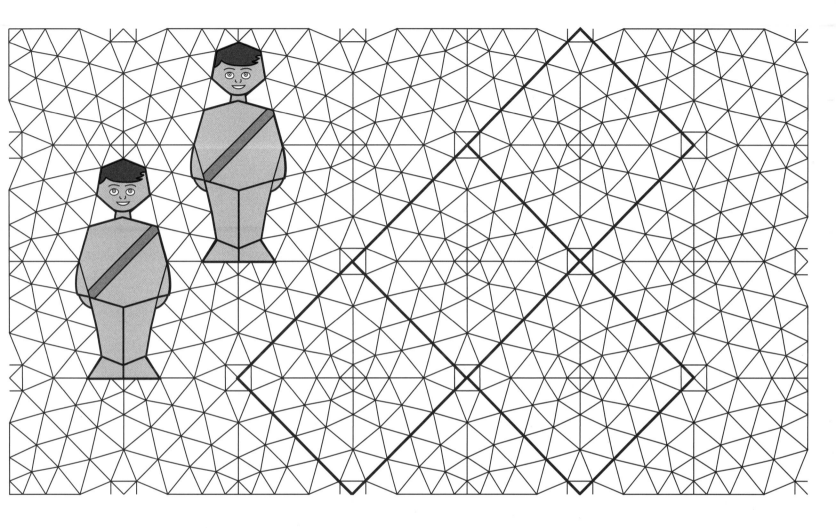

All of the designs in this book are based on close-packing circles. Four close-packed circles are positioned within a 45-degree, right-angle triangle. The triangle is reflected and rotated to create a square, and the square tessellates to cover the plane.

DESIGN # 1

In each design you will find simple shapes that repeat, just like the small squares above. You will find that an image, like the knight in armor, will repeat and rotate around these simple shapes. See if you can find the squares and the knight in the design on the right.

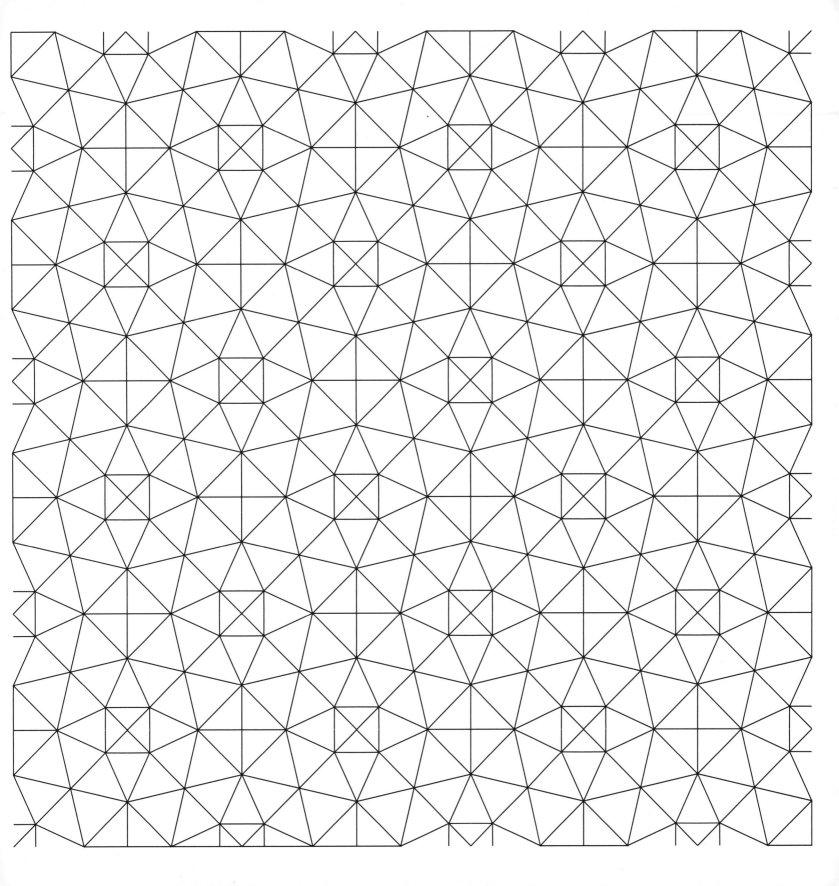

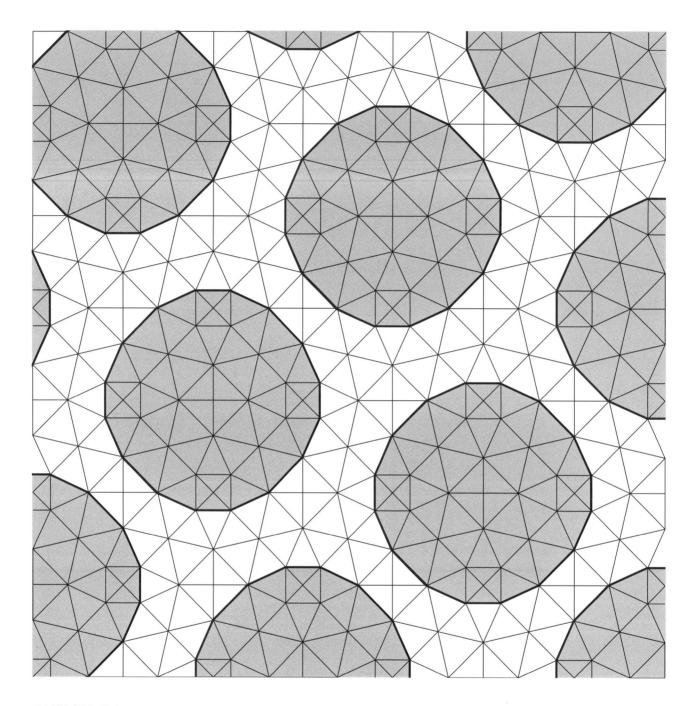

DESIGN # 1

These sixteen-sided shapes repeat all over the design. Can you find them in the design on the right? Can you transform them with color and your imagination?

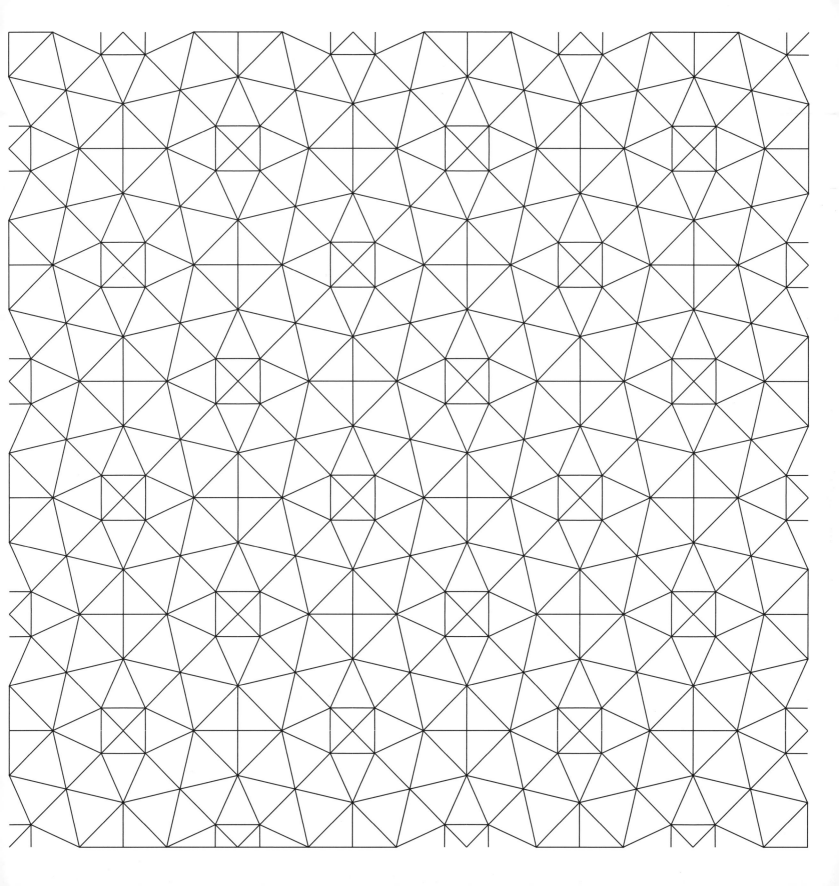

DESIGN # 1

A gryphon is a legendary creature with the body of a lion and the head and wings of an eagle. In legends the gryphon guards something priceless. See if you can find these gryphons in the design on the right.

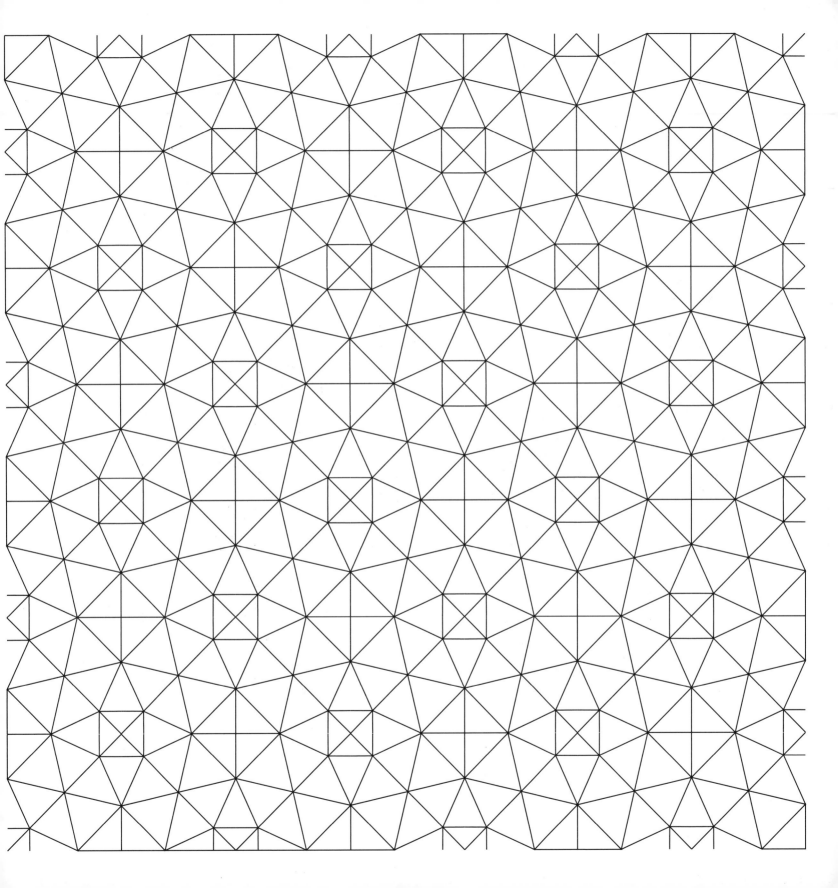

DESIGN # 1

You can create complete scenes with the images you find. Here is a complete scene with a gryphon and knights.

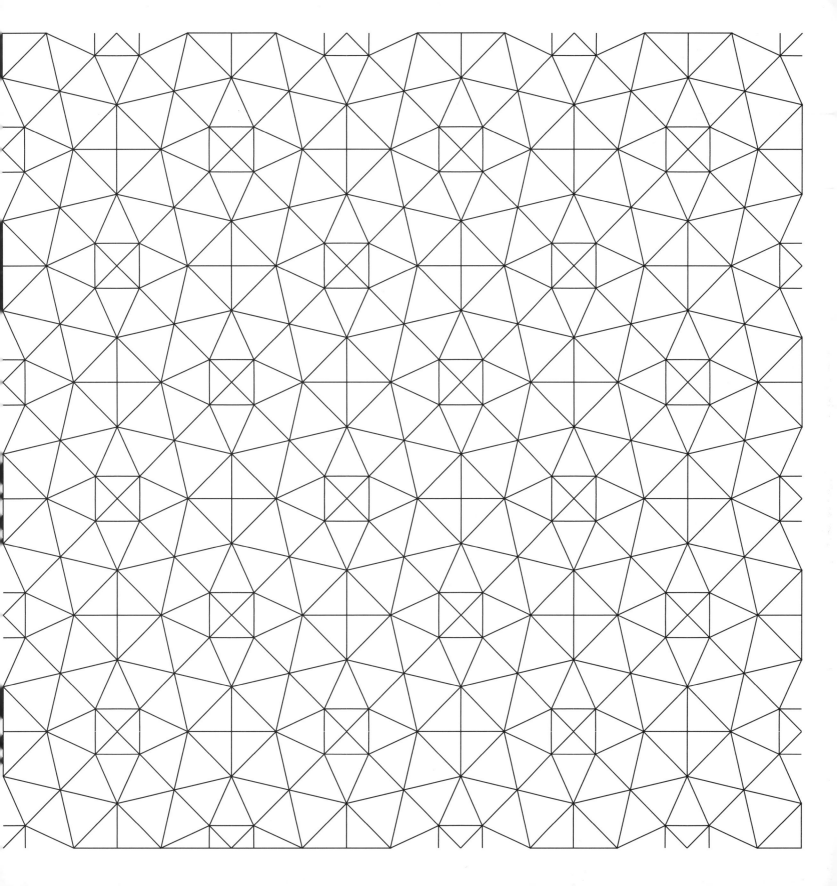

DESIGN # 2

When you find the repeating squares you will be able to find the dragons, knights, and princesses in the design on the right.

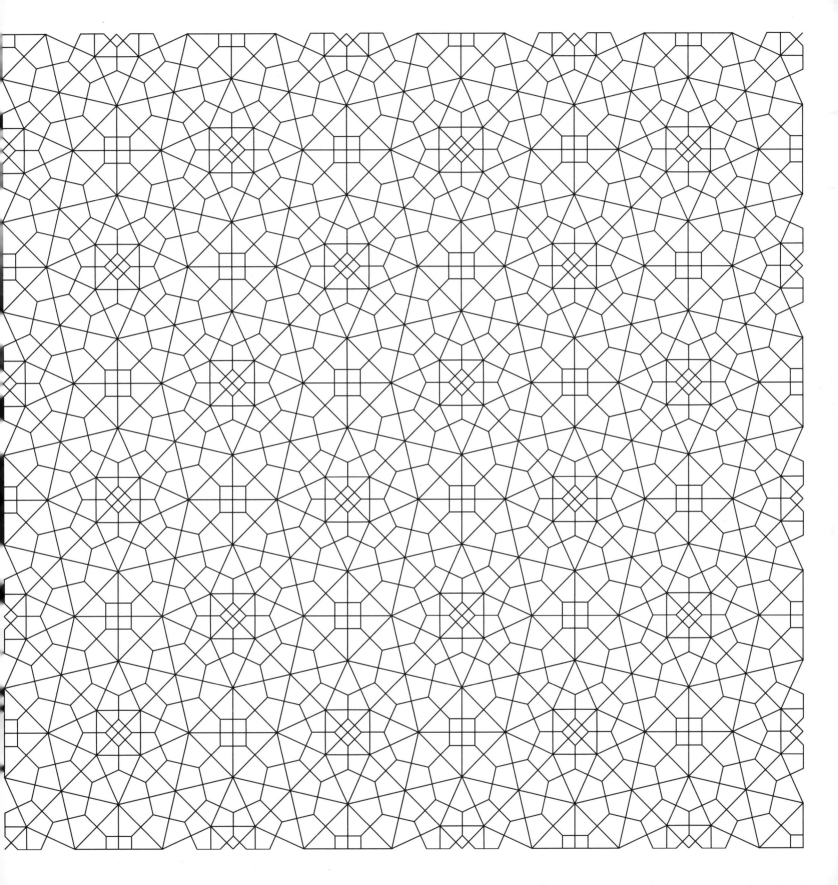

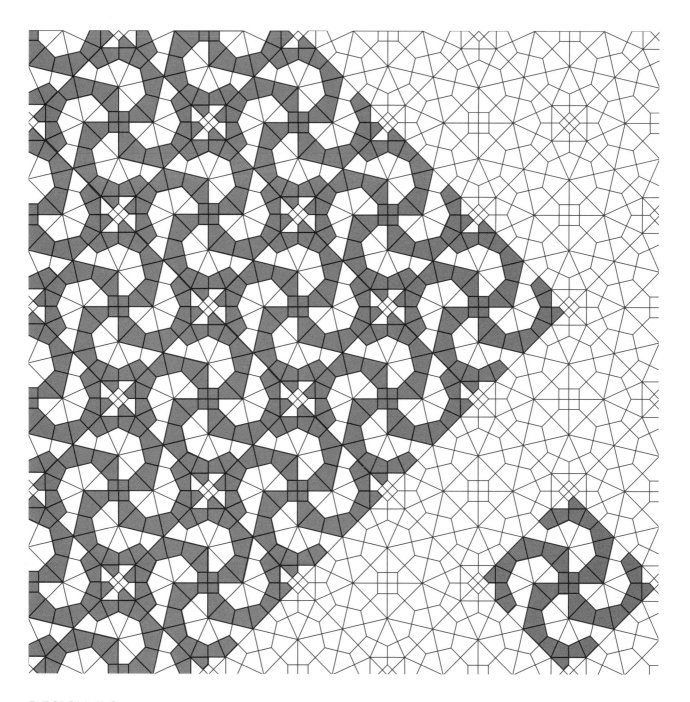

DESIGN # 2

Look for the repeating squares. When you find them you should be able to find the spiral shape. The spiral shape repeats to cover the whole design.

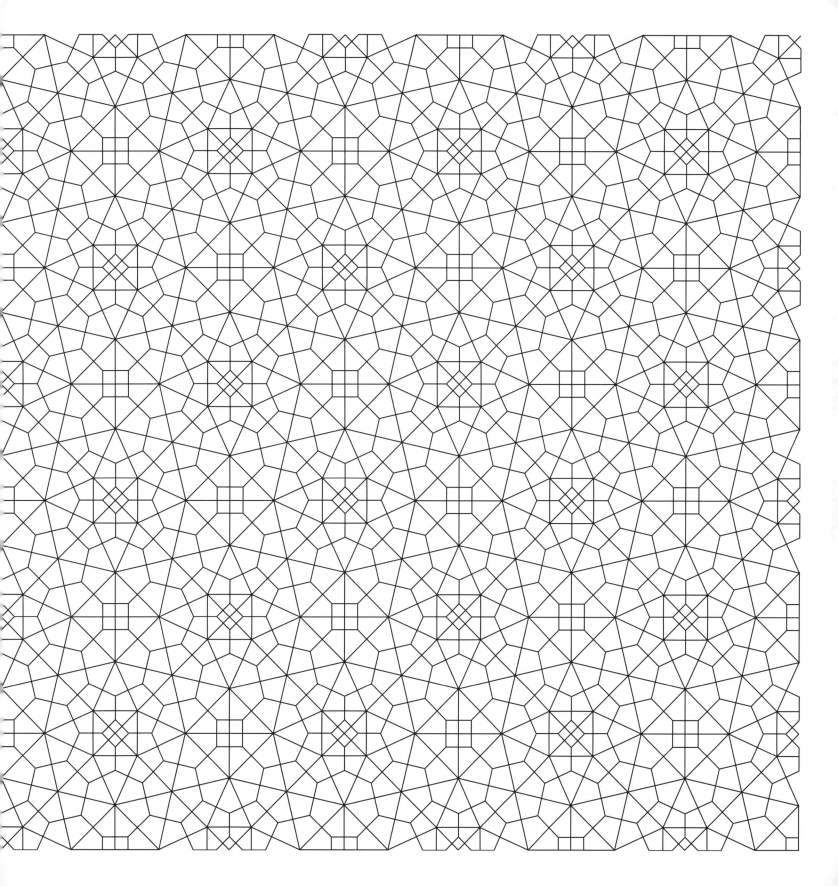

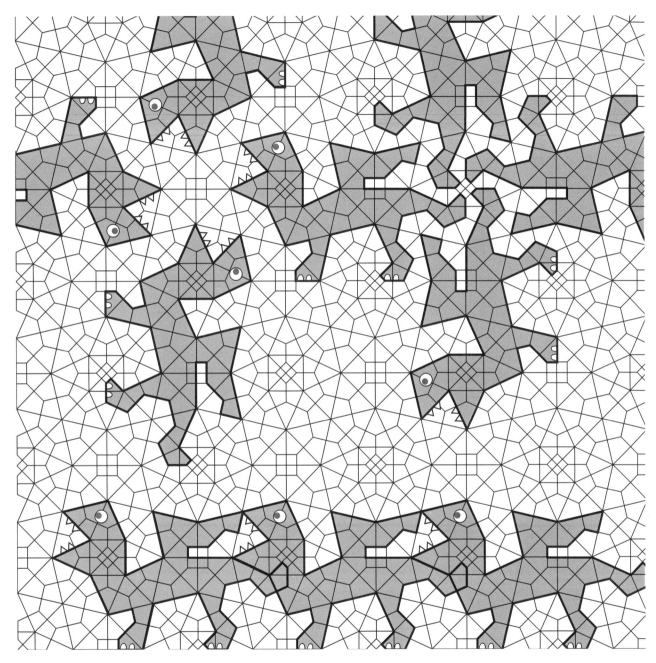

DESIGN # 2
See how the dragons repeat and rotate around the squares. Can you make up your own dragon pattern?

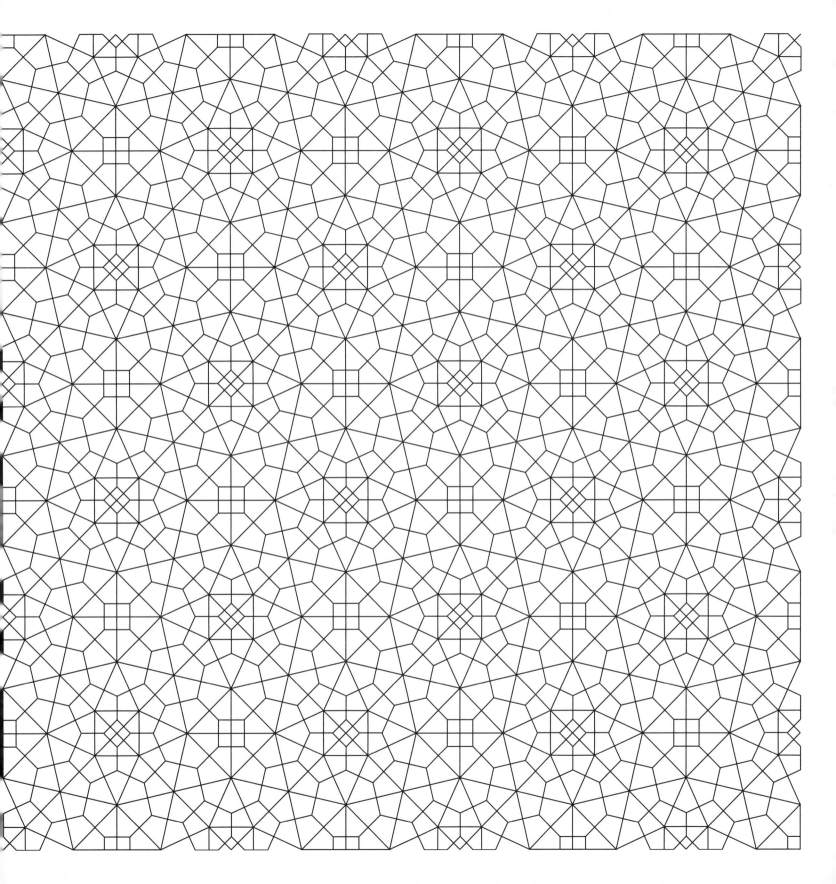

DESIGN # 2

Combine the princesses with knights and dragons to build a scene.

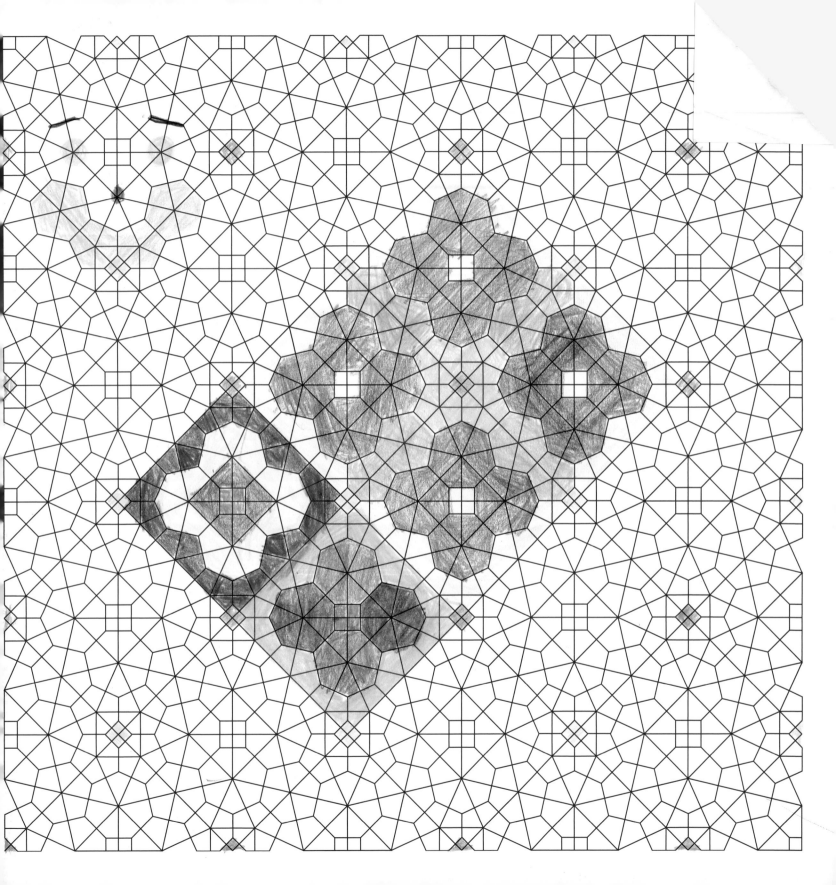

DESIGN # 3

Find the fairies next to the squares.

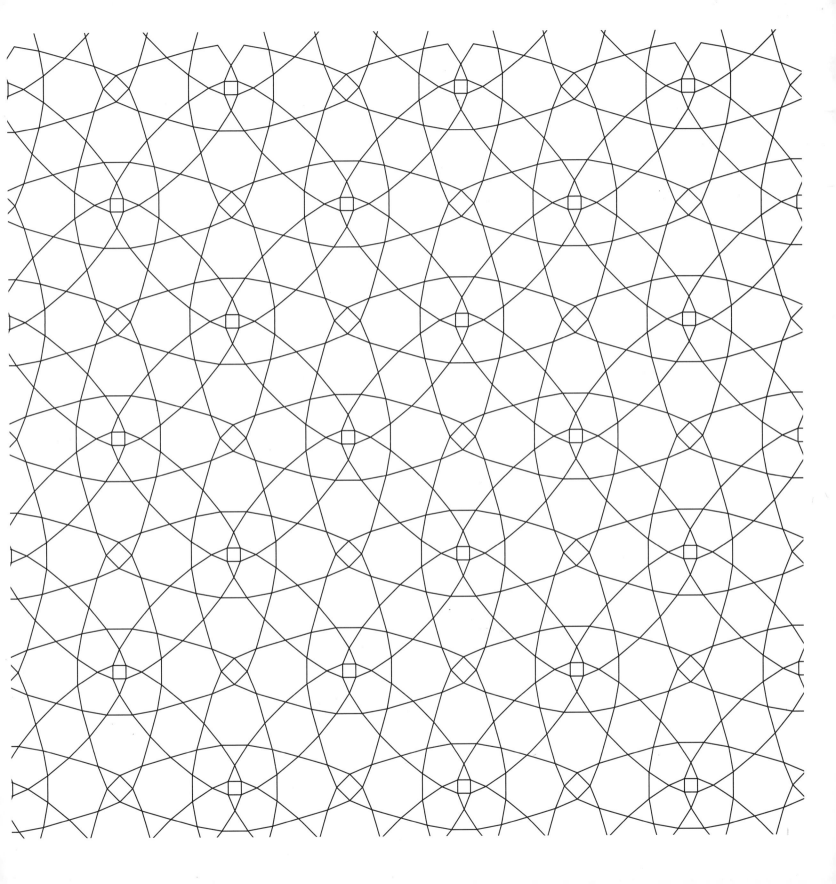

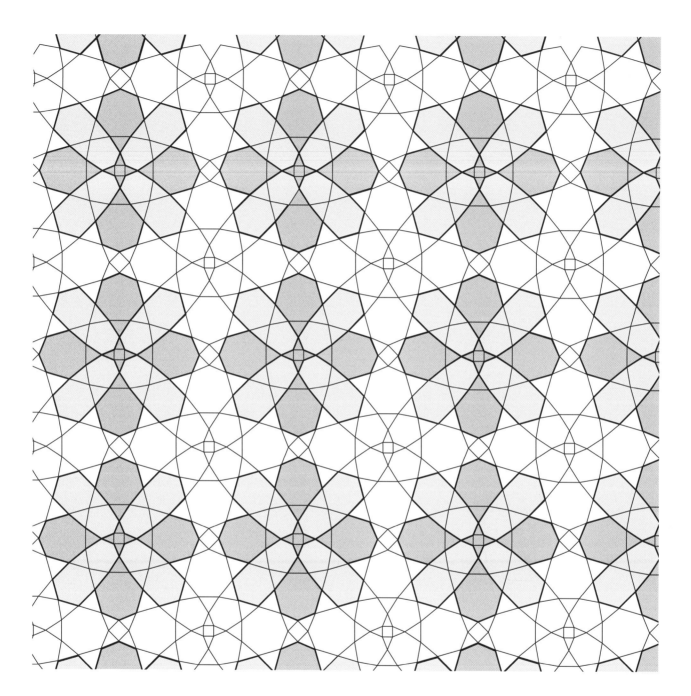

DESIGN # 3

The flowers repeat to make a pattern.

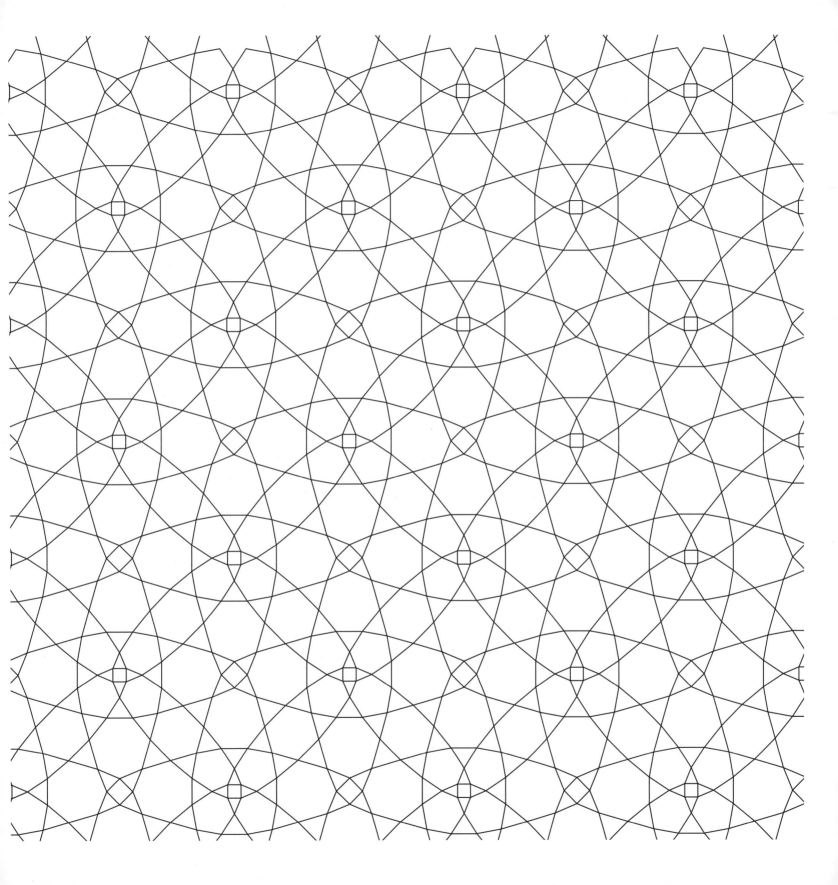

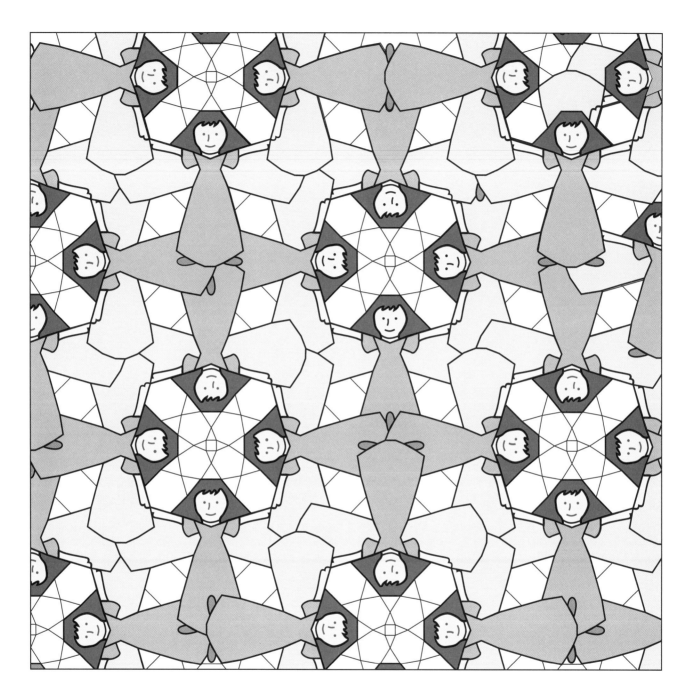

DESIGN # 3

The fairies repeat to make a pattern.

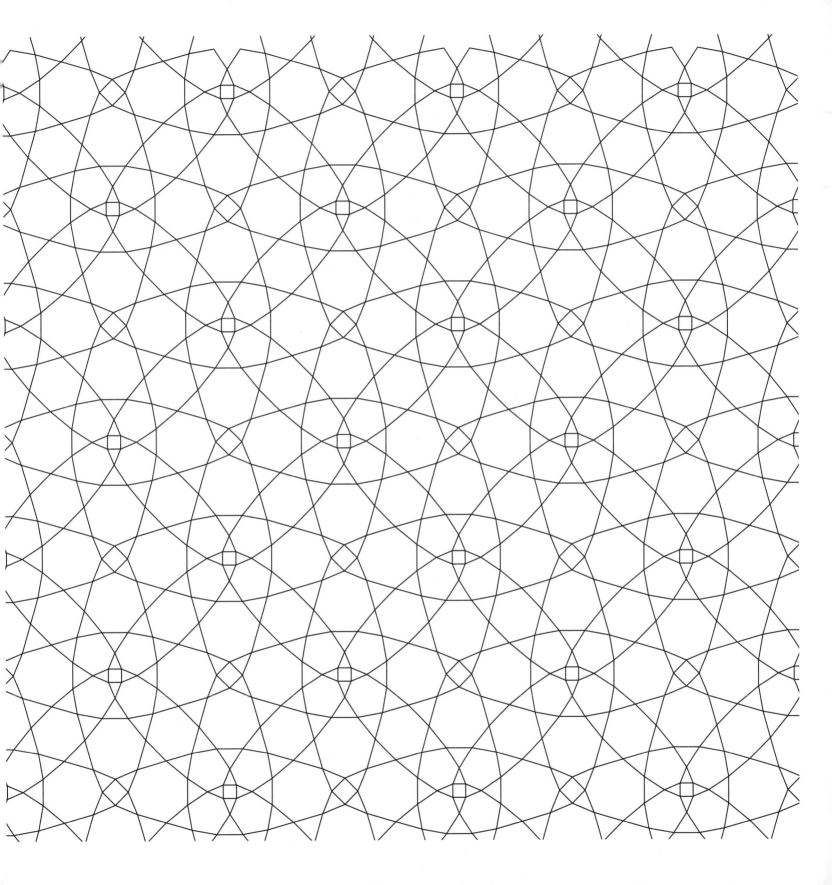

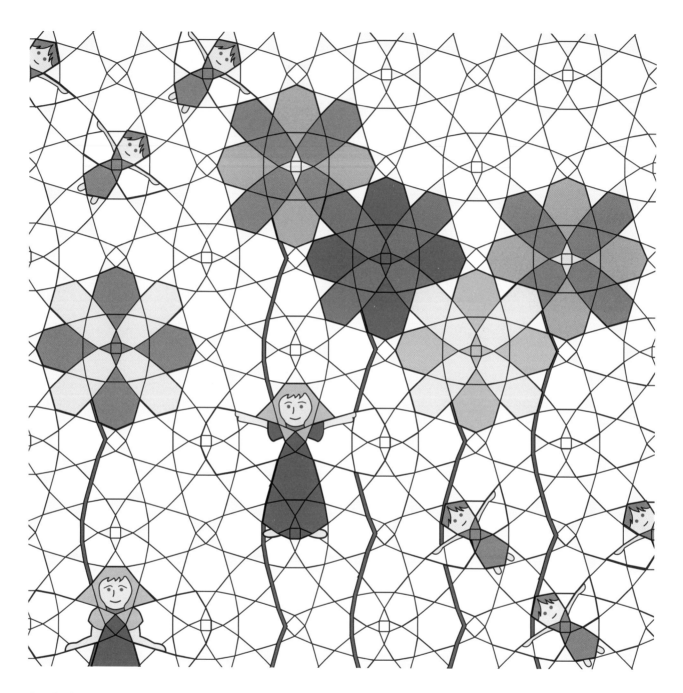

DESIGN # 3

Combine the fairies and flowers to make a scene of your own.

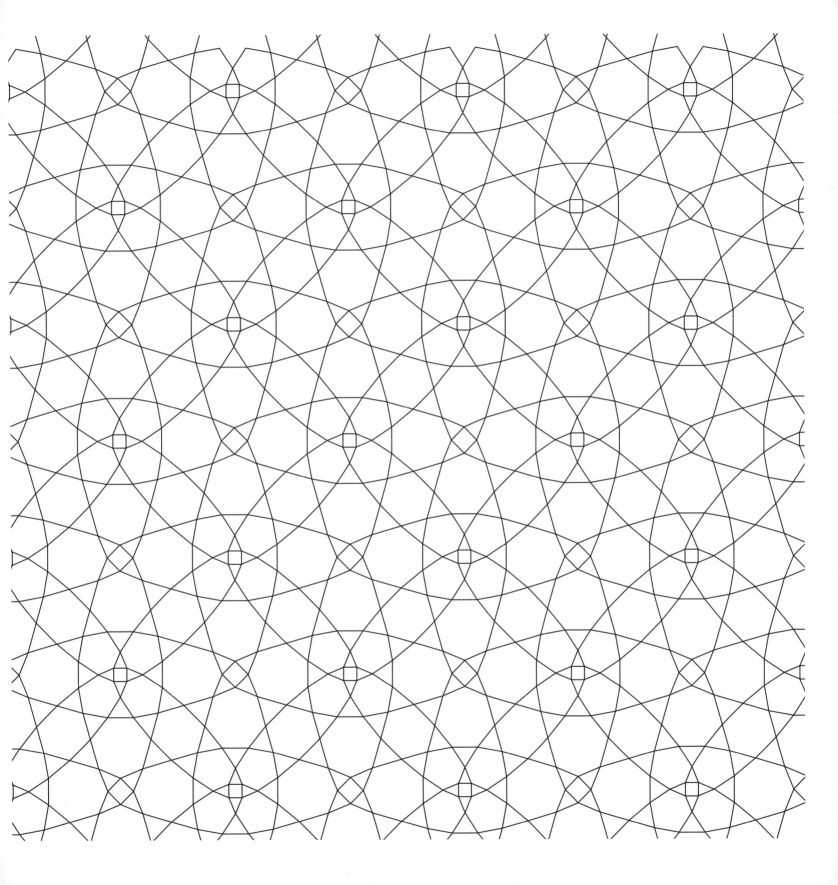

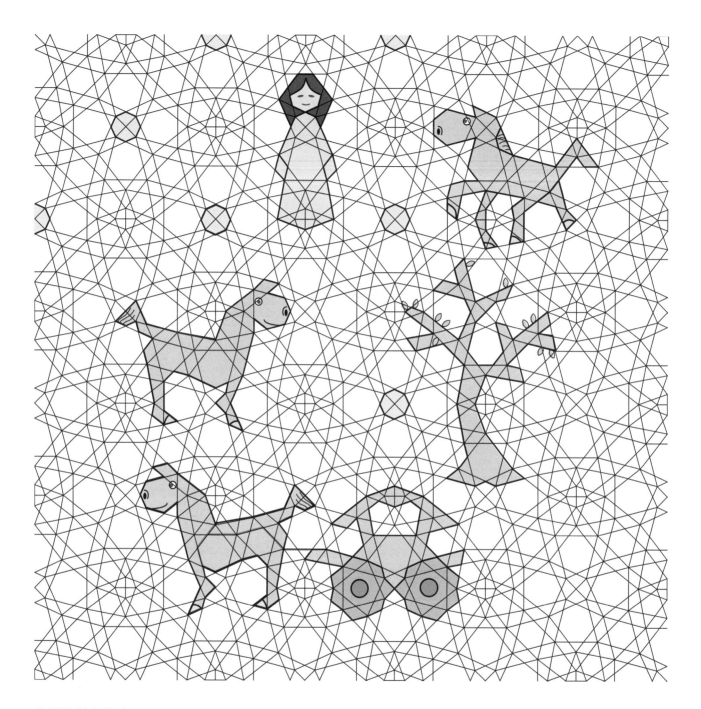

DESIGN # 4

The princess and horses repeat next to the octagons.

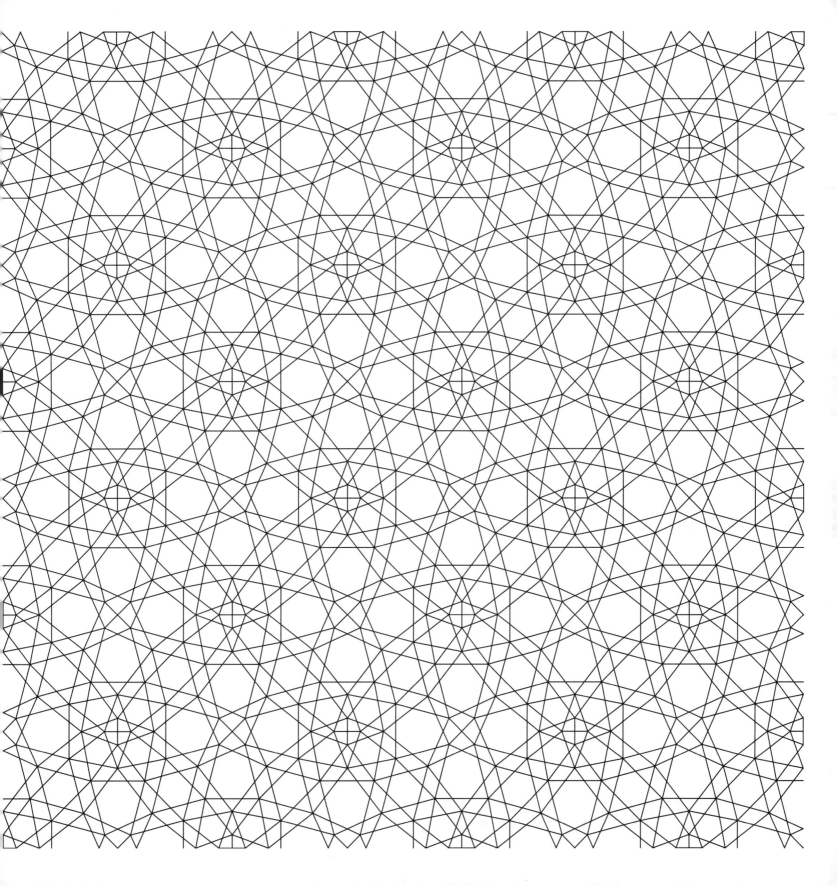

DESIGN # 4

Find the repeating octagons and then see if you can find the wavy lines to build this pattern.

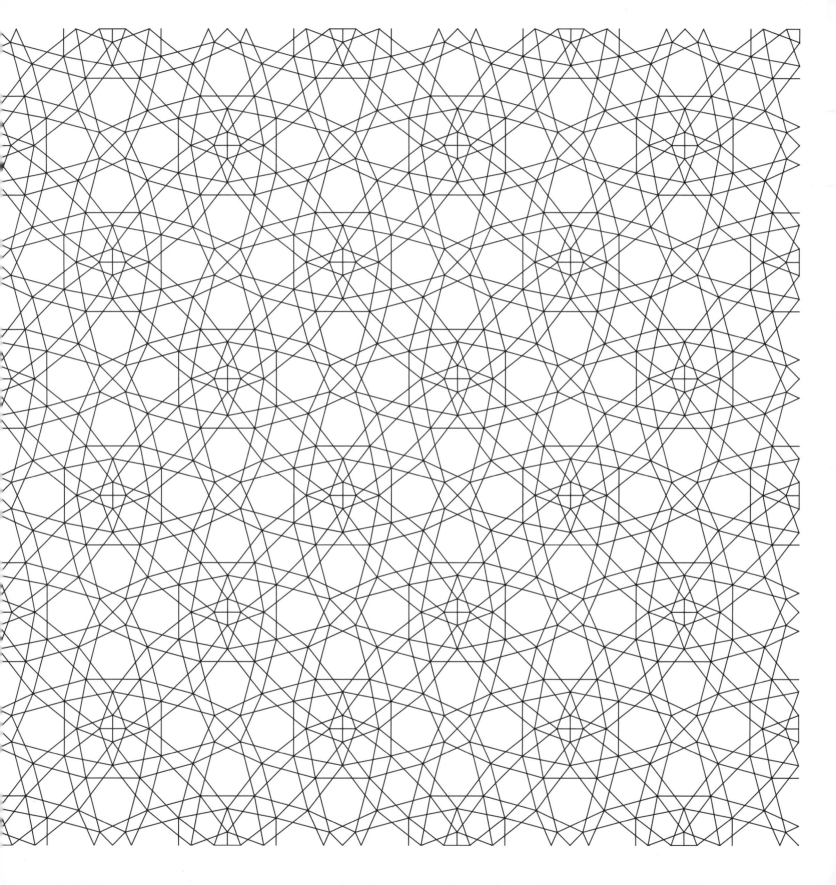

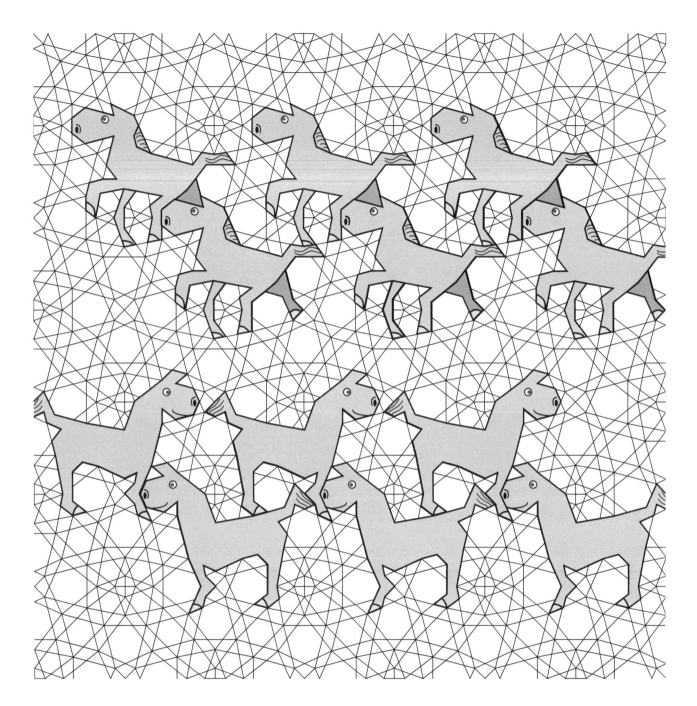

DESIGN # 4

The horses repeat next to the octagons, and they will also rotate around them.

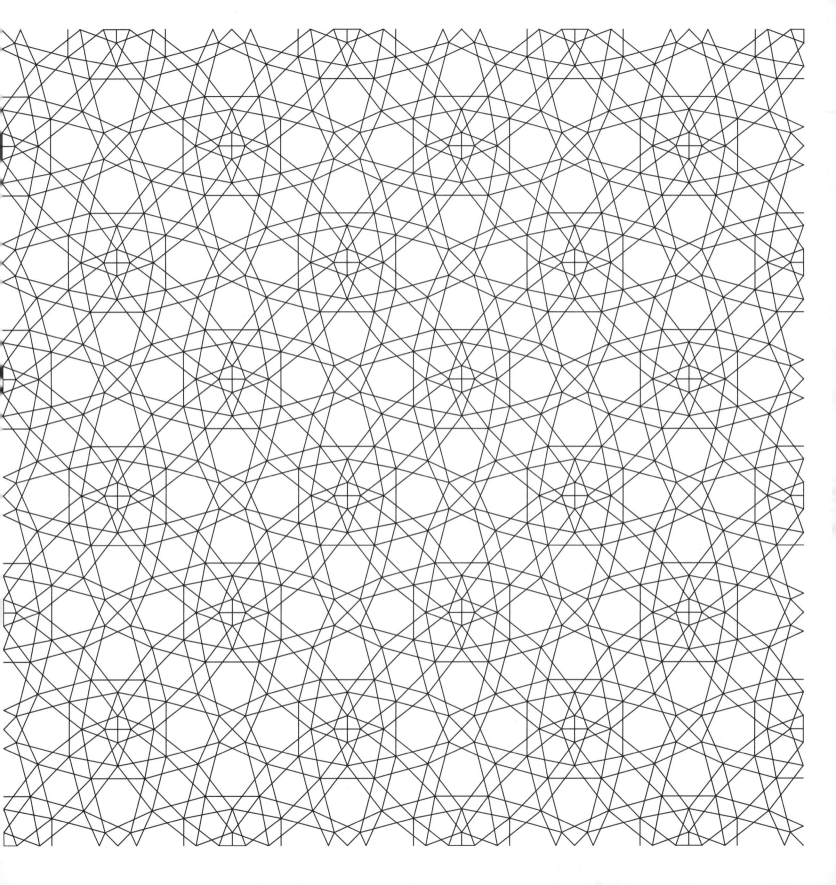

DESIGN # 4

Combine the images of the princess, horses, and trees to build a scene of your own.

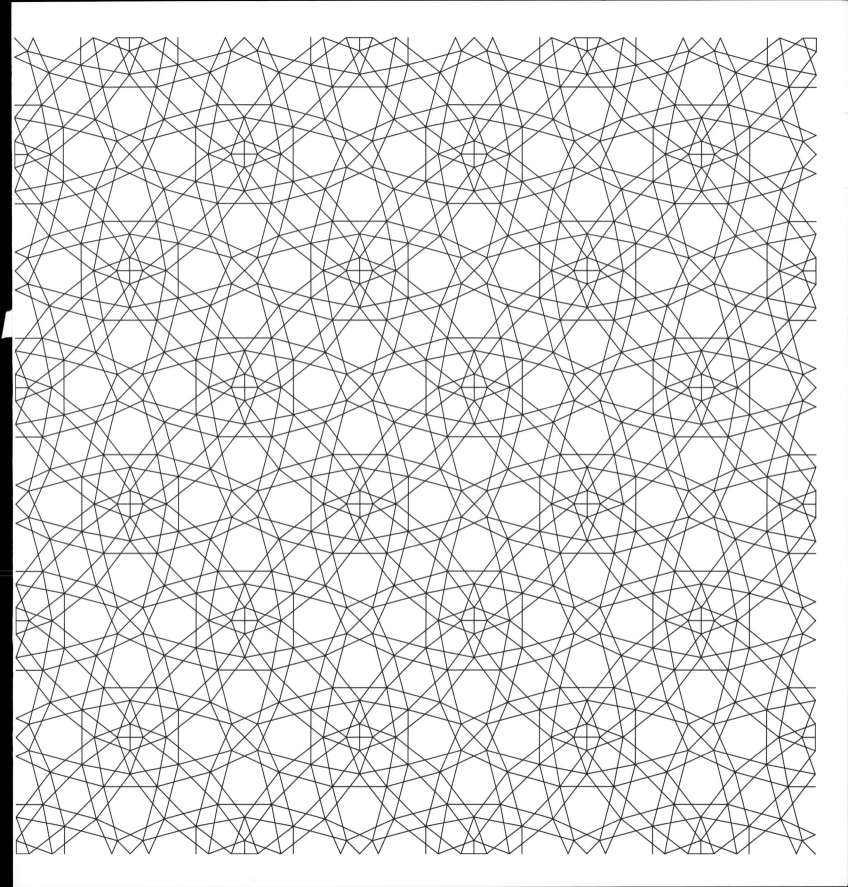

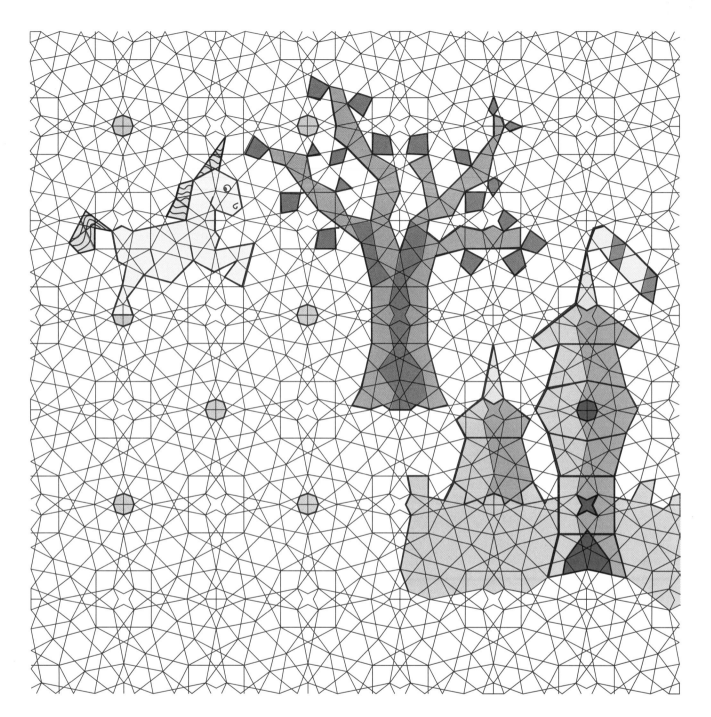

DESIGN # 5

Look for the repeating octagons and find the unicorn, tree, and castle.

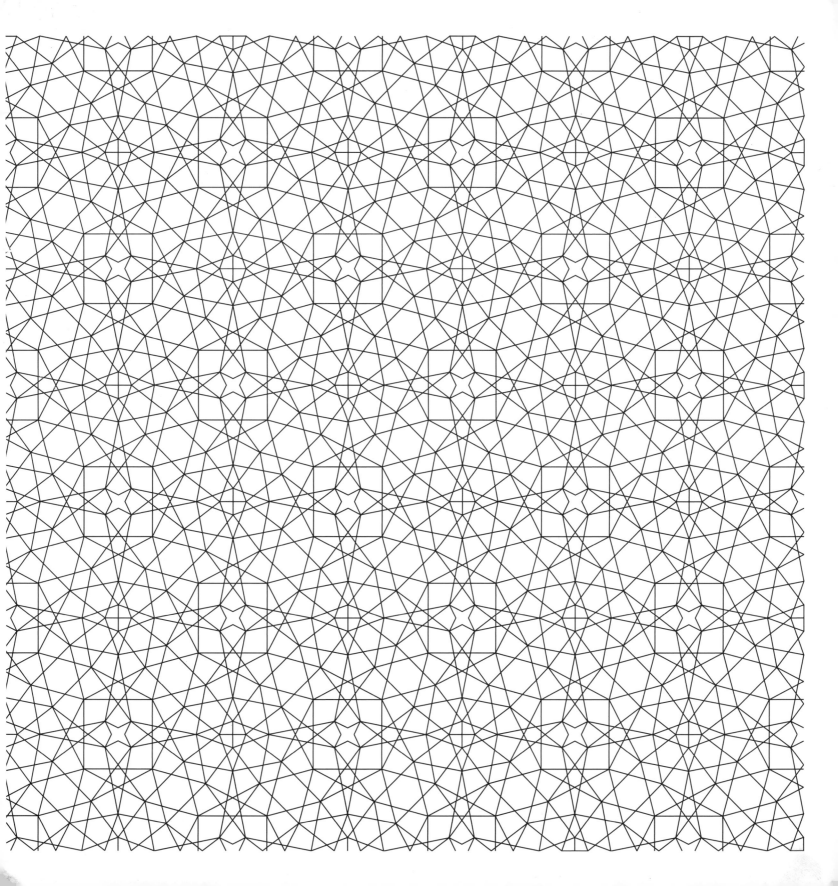

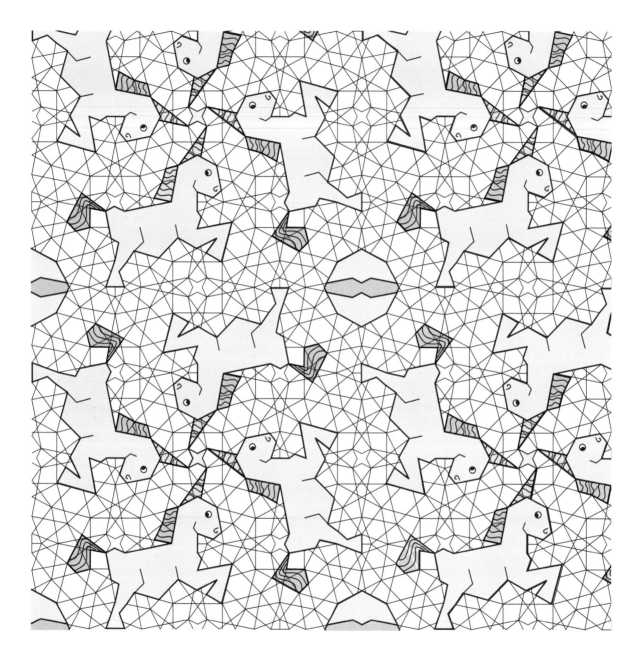

DESIGN # 5

The unicorns rotate around the four-sided stars to create this pattern.

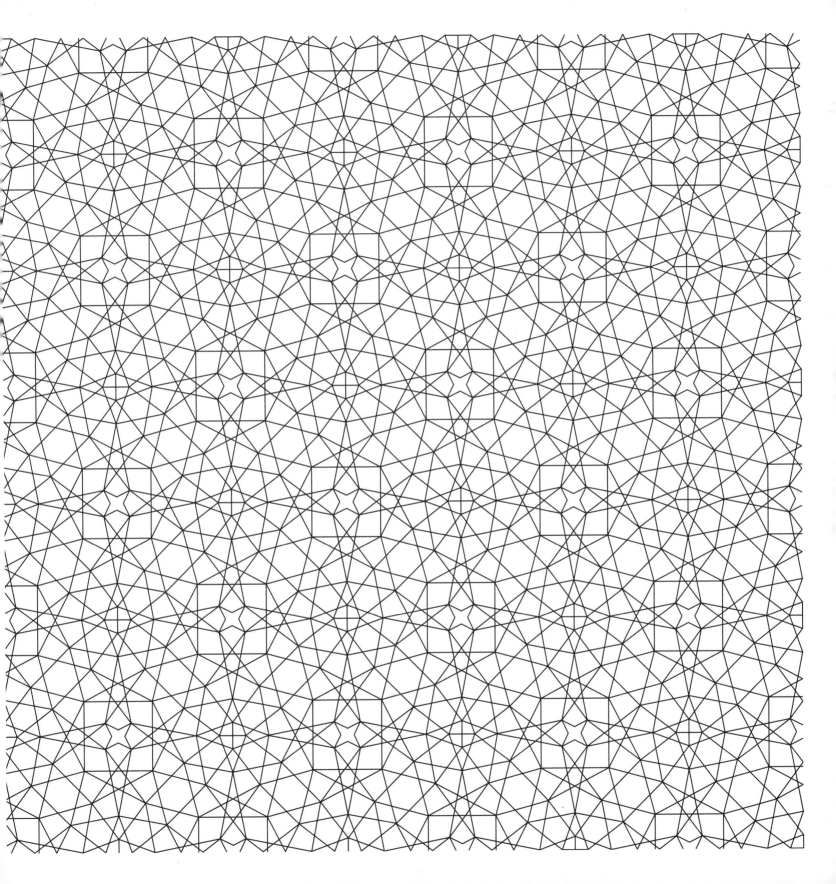

DESIGN # 5

Here's a finished scene combining unicorns, a tree, and a castle. Place images in your own way to create your own scene on the right.

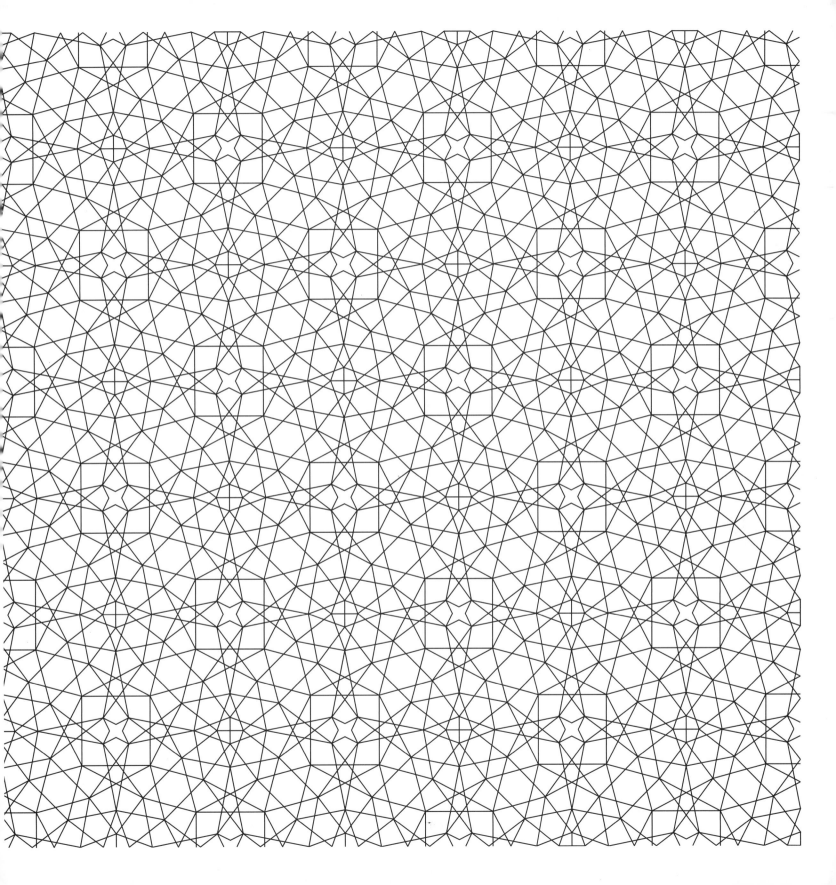

DESIGN # 6

Find the four-sided stars and then see if you can find the other images in the design on the right.

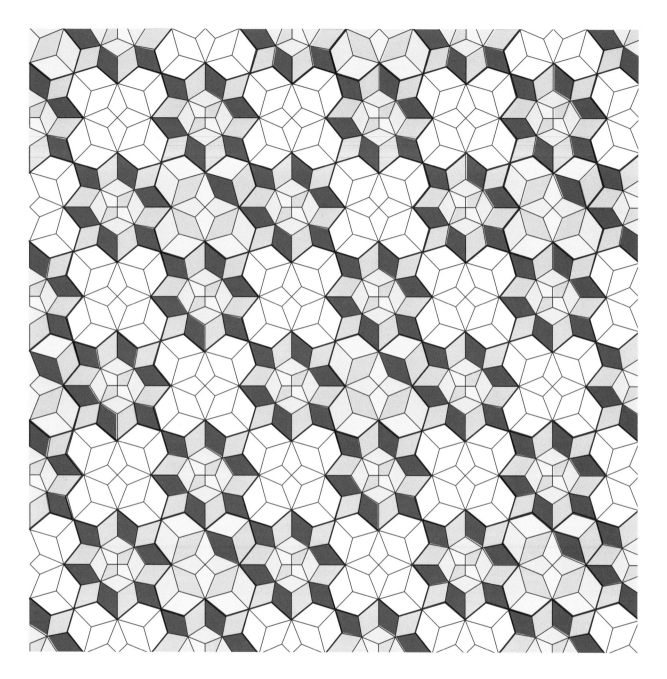

DESIGN # 6

The eight-sided star shape repeats to create this pattern.

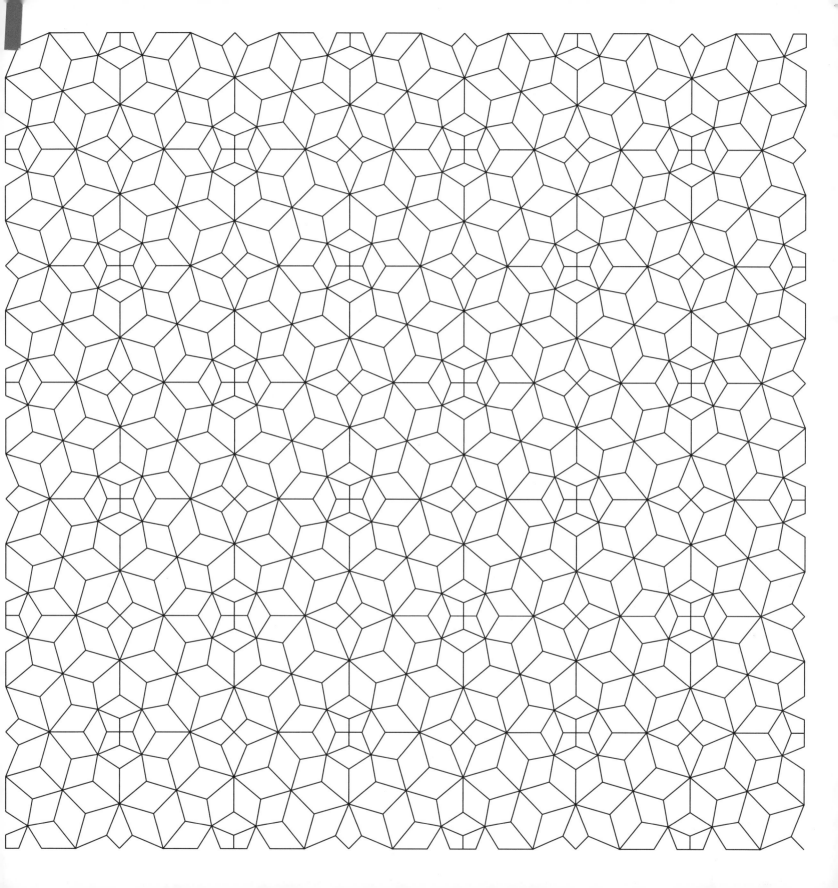

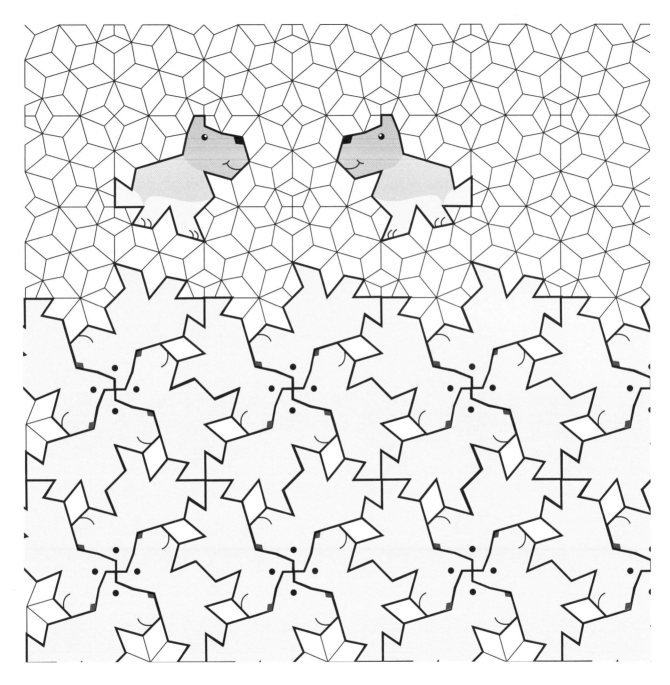

DESIGN # 6

Find the images of the dogs and then see in what ways you can repeat them to create a pattern.

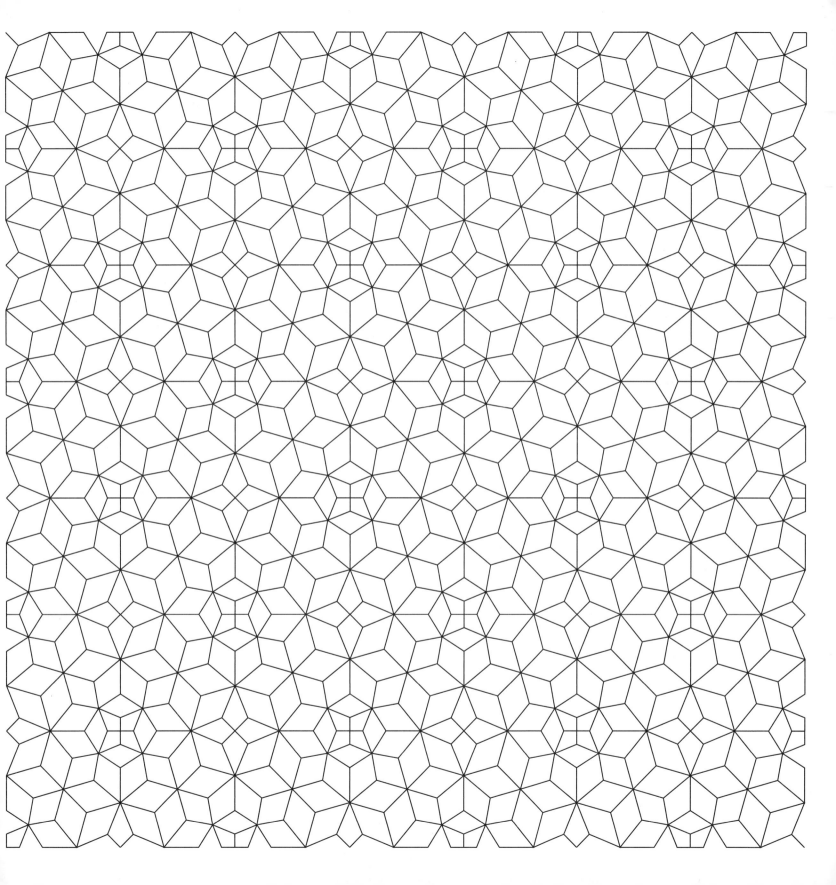

DESIGN # 6

Combine the images of the queen, fairies, and dogs to create a complete scene.

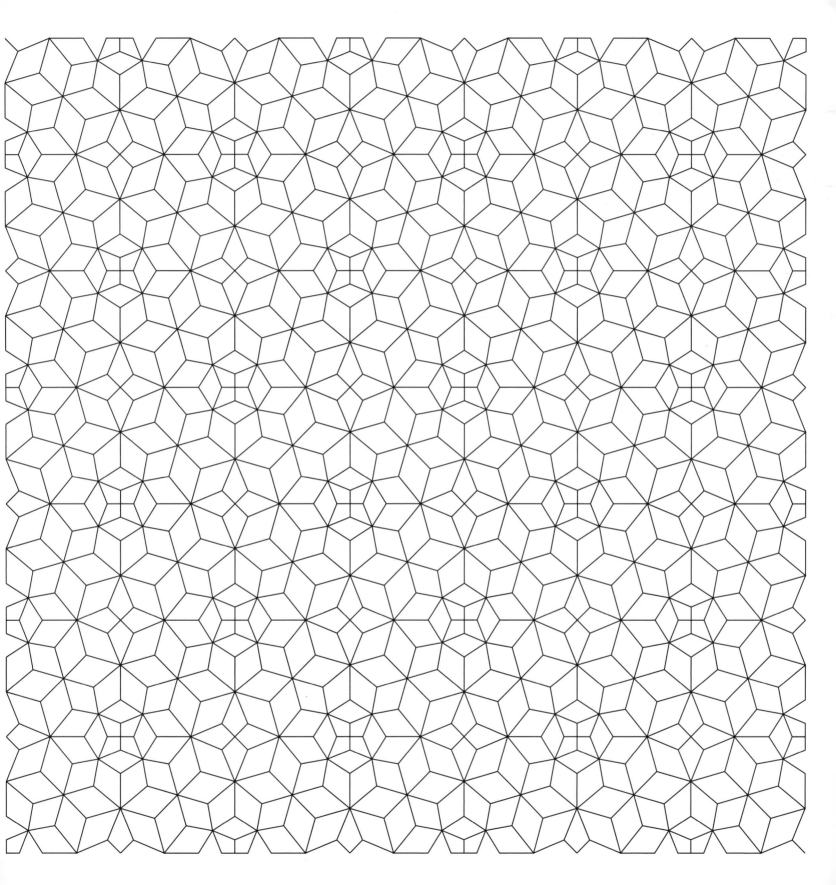

DESIGN # 7

Find the repeating four-sided stars in the design on the right. Then find the images of the dancing prince and princess.

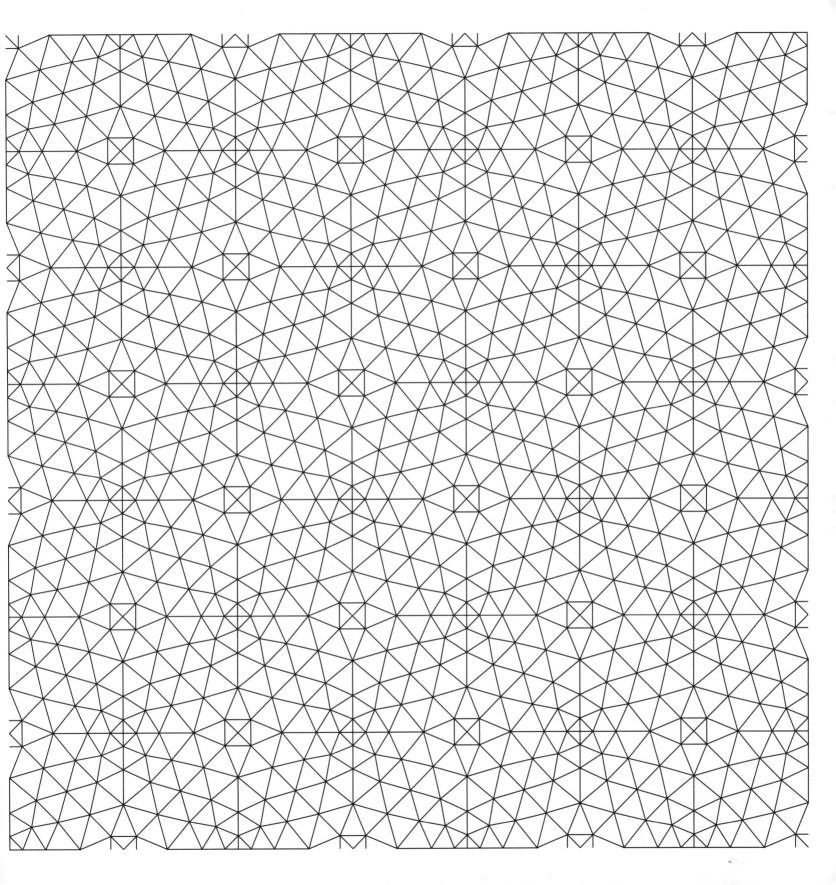

DESIGN # 7

Repeat these circular shapes to create a pattern of your own. What can you see?

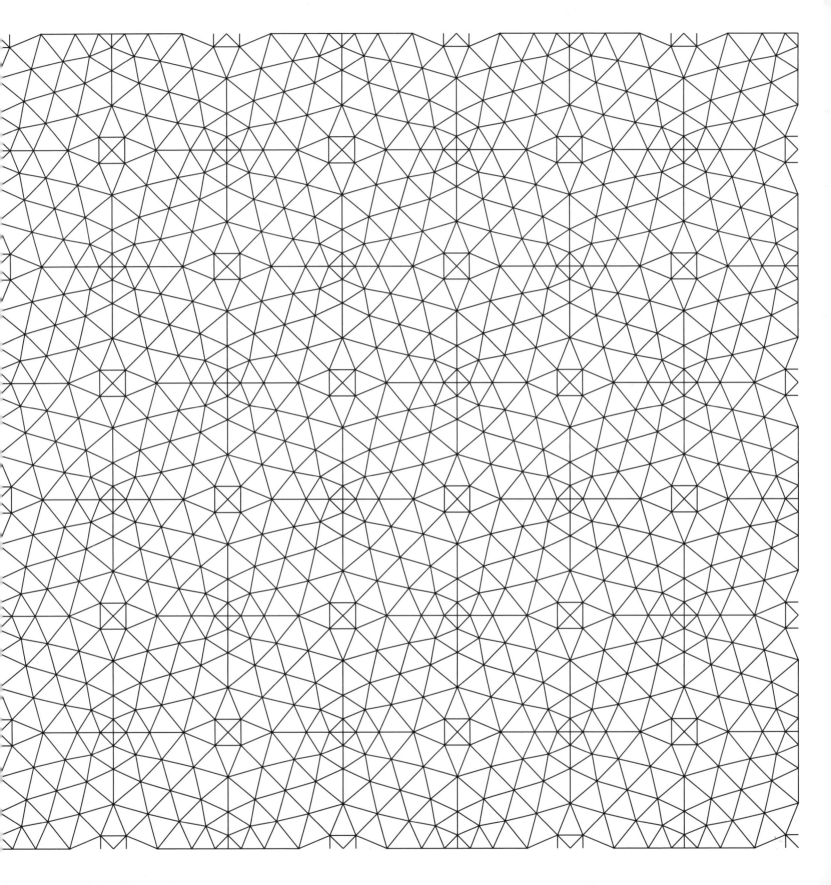

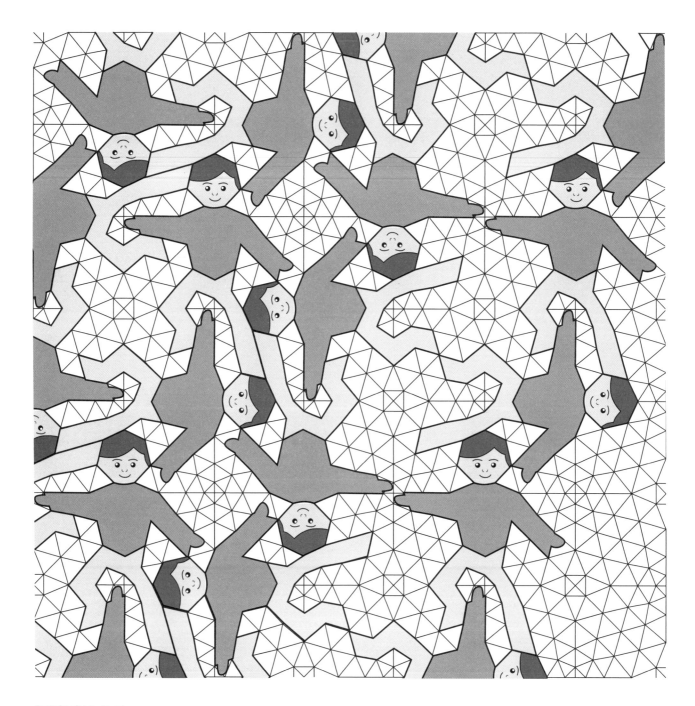

DESIGN # 7

Images of the dancing prince can be combined to create a pattern.

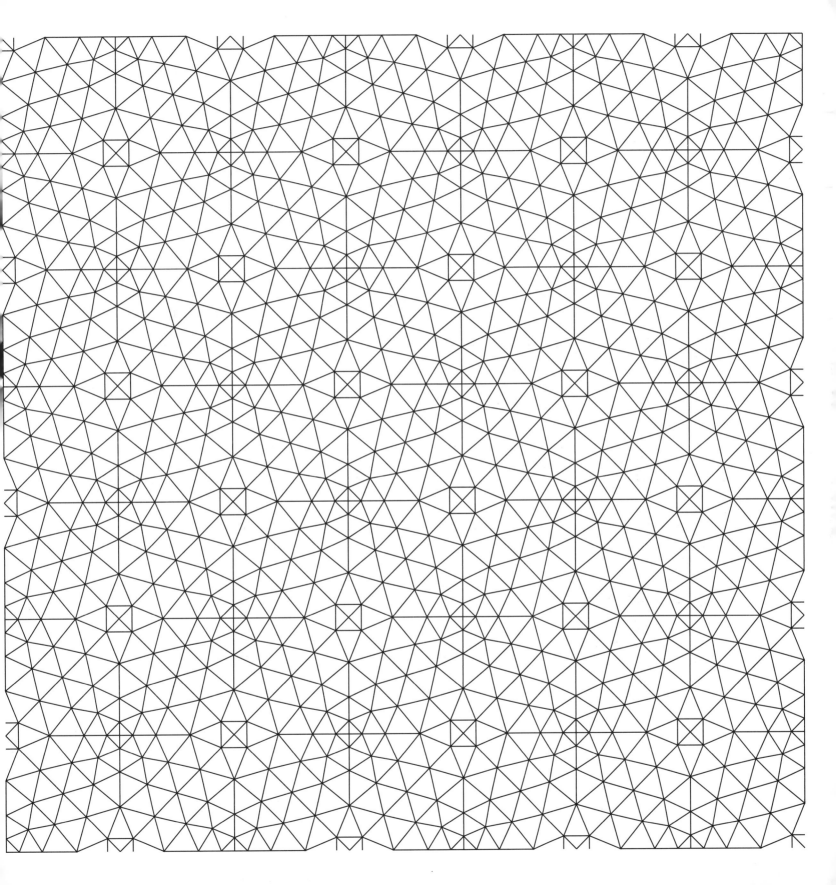

DESIGN # 7

Create a complete scene with all the images you find.

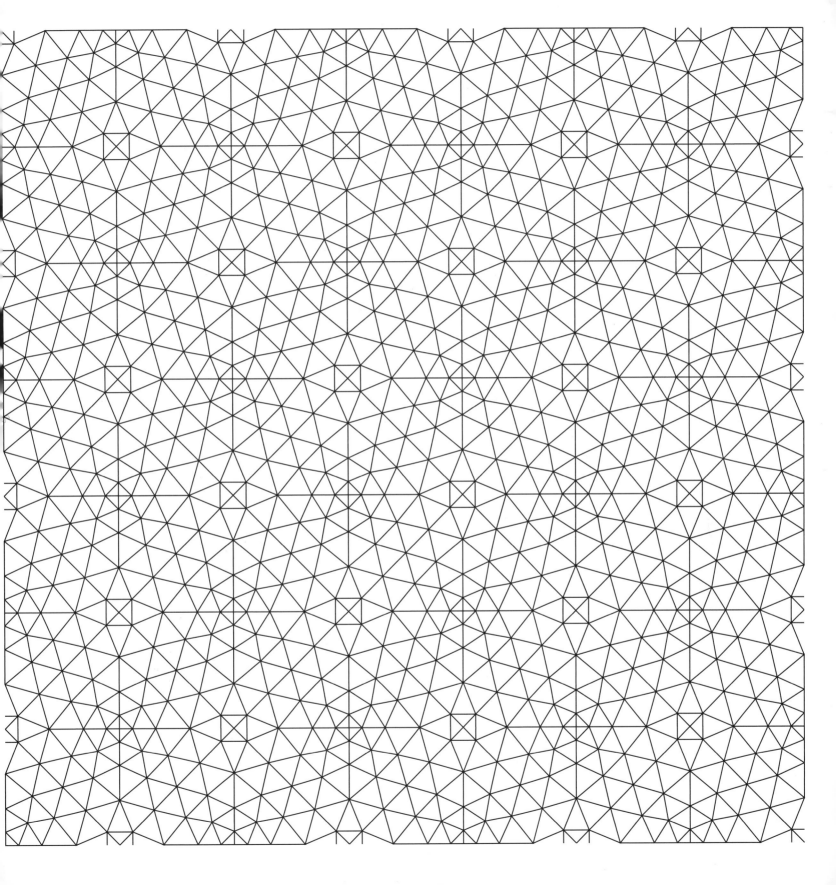

DESIGN # 8

What images can you see in the design on the right?

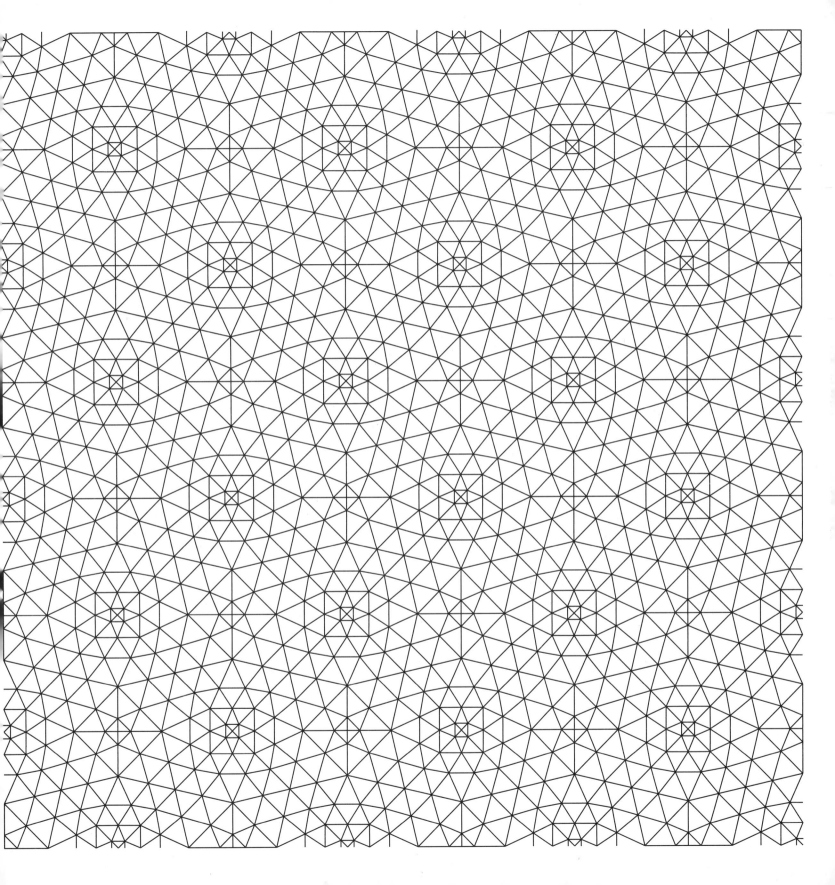

DESIGN # 8

The spiral shape above repeats to create an interlocking pattern. What patterns can you find?

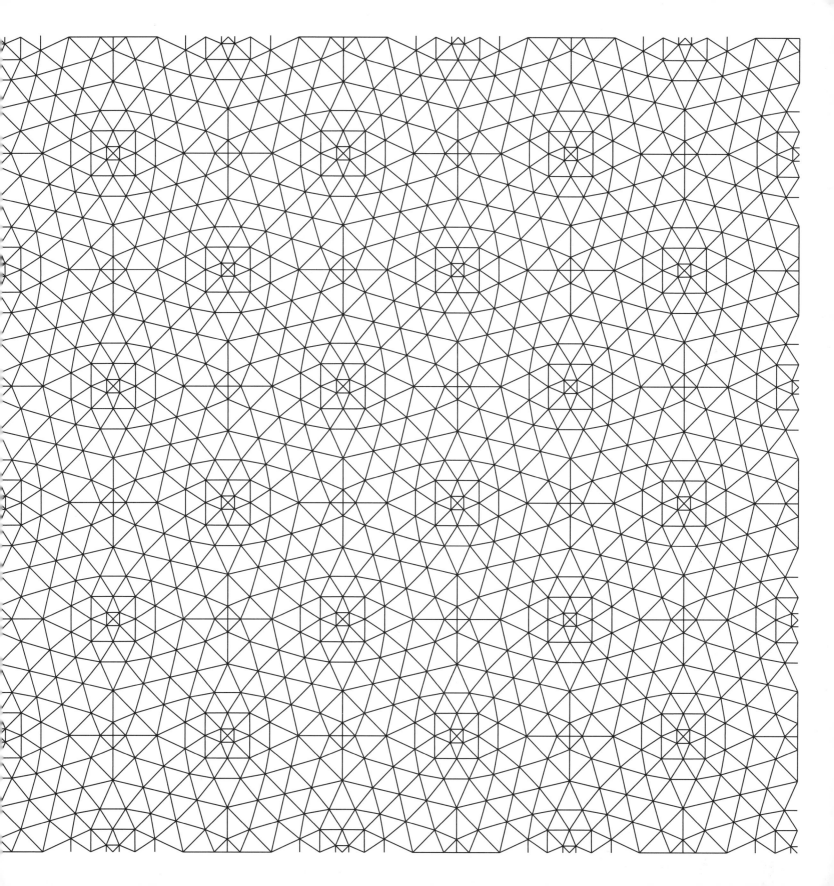

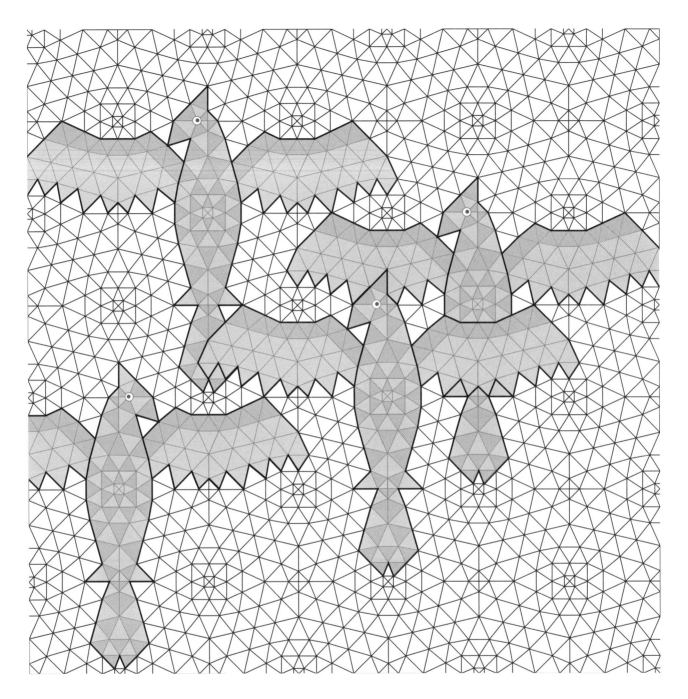

DESIGN # 8

The phoenix is a bird born from fire. See how the phoenix repeats above to create a pattern.

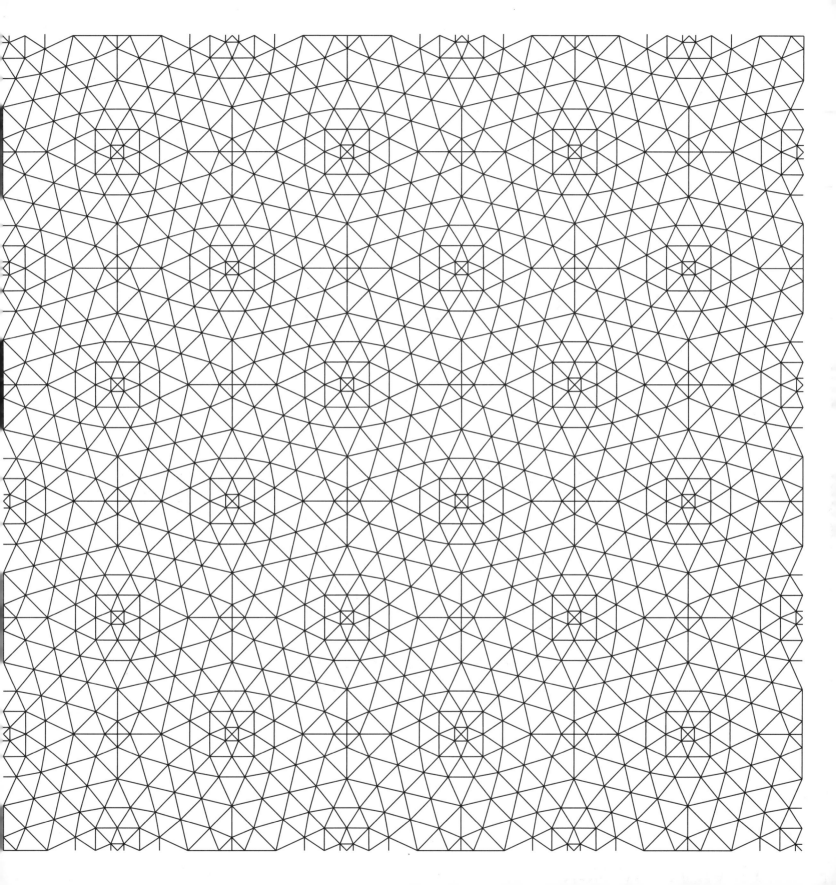

DESIGN # 8

Create a complete scene with the images you find.

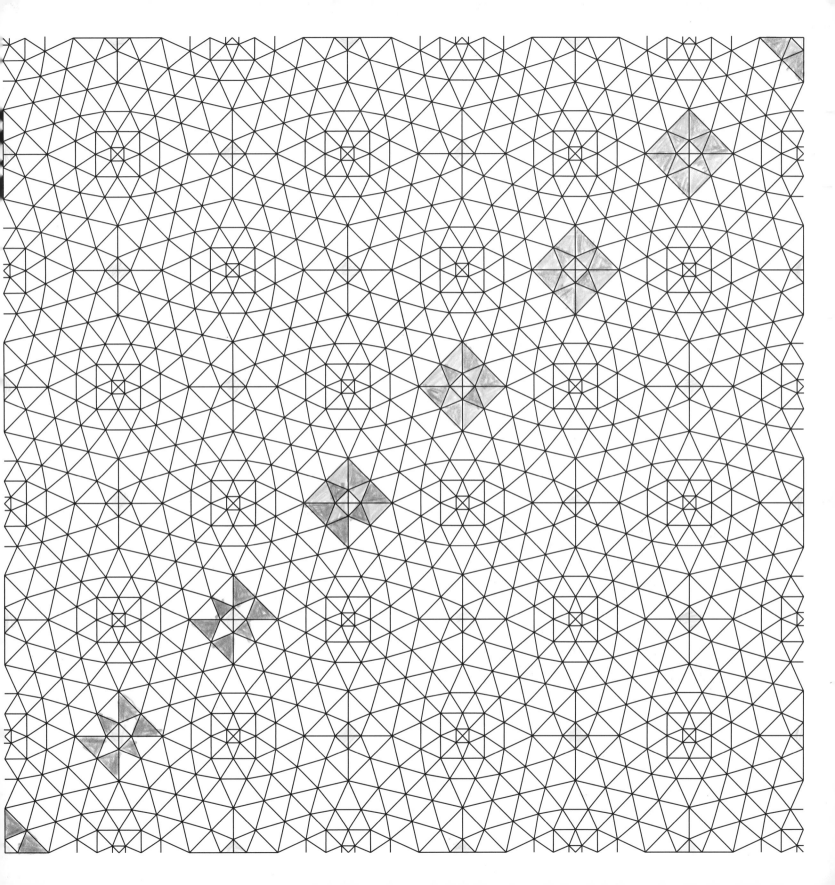

DESIGN # 9

Find the repeating octagons and then look for the wizard, owl, and dog.

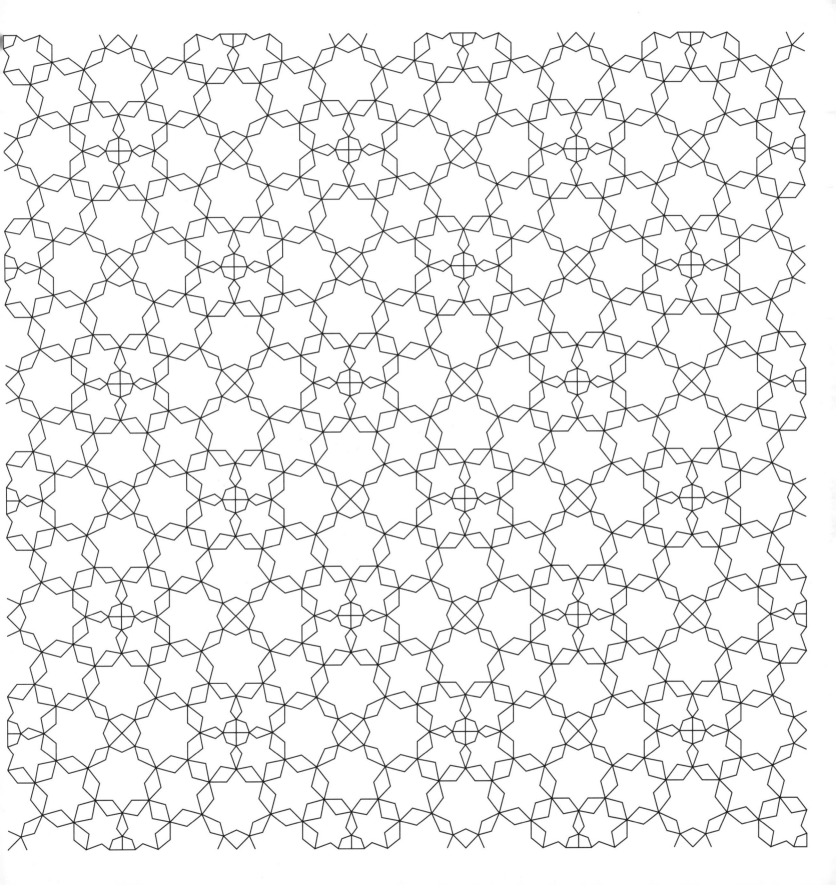

DESIGN # 9

Here's a centered design like a mandala. Start by finding the octagon and then build the design around it.

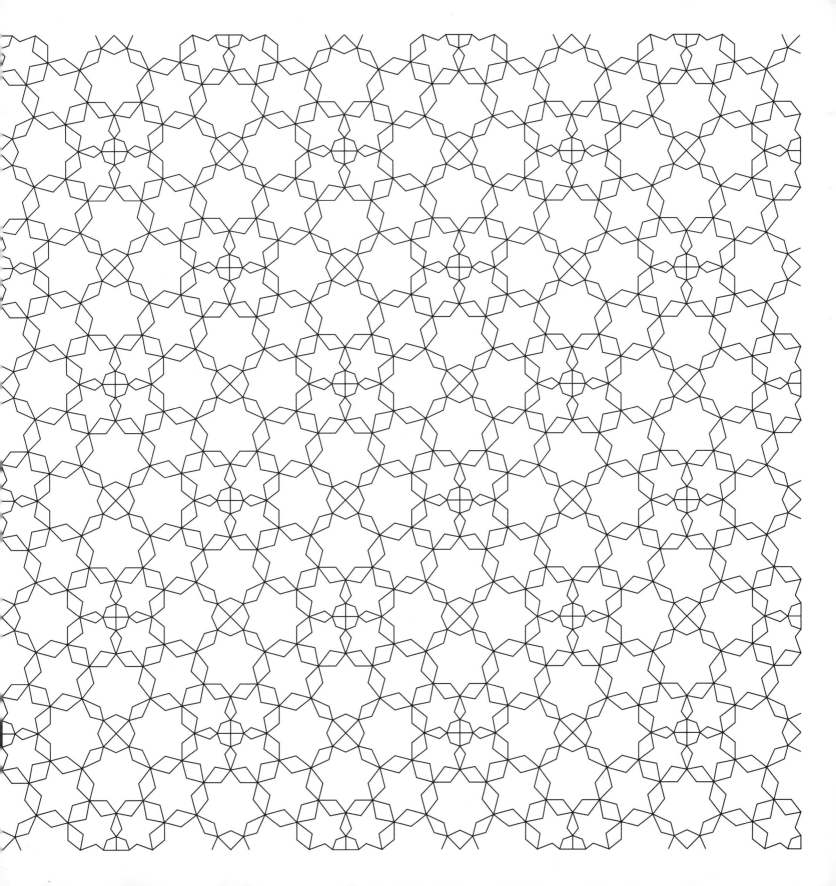

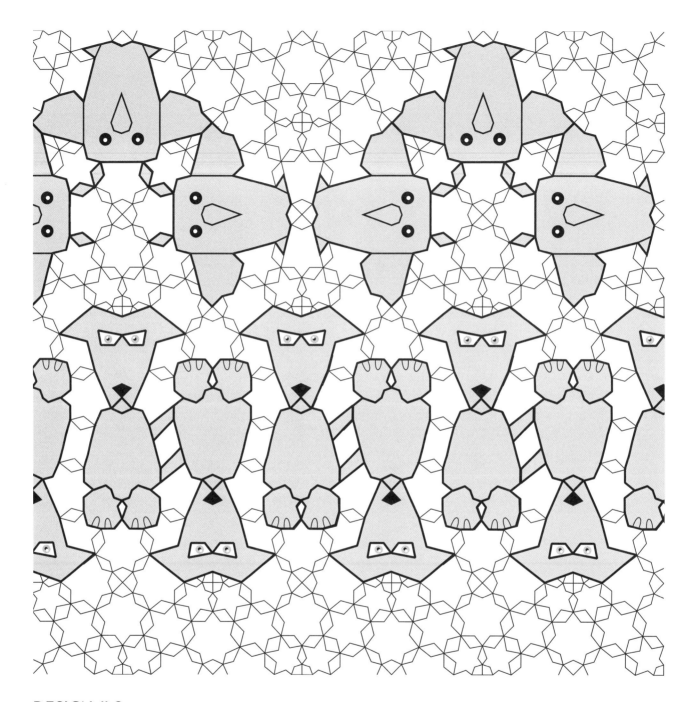

DESIGN # 9

The dogs and owls can be repeated in different ways to create a pattern.

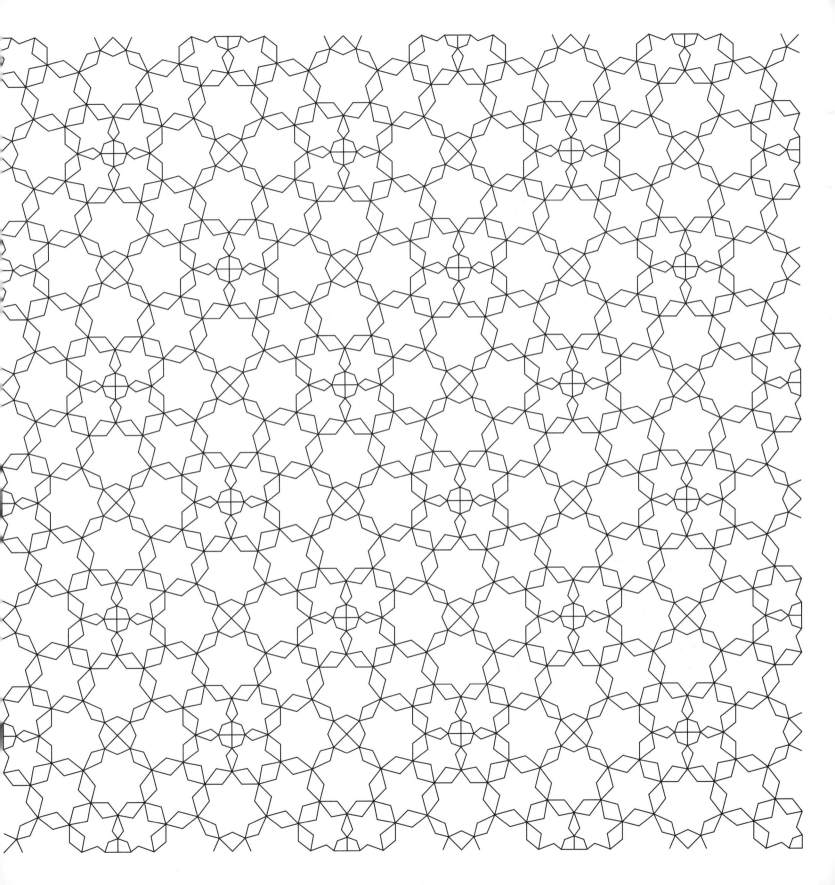

DESIGN # 9

Create a complete scene with the images you find.

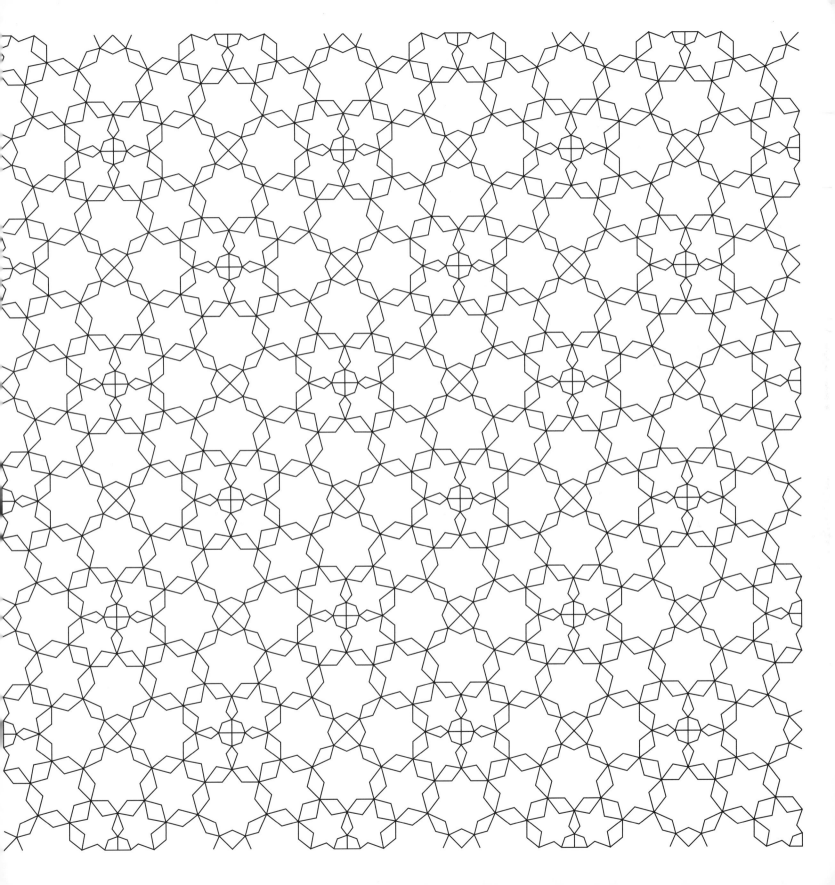

DESIGN # 10

Find the octagons and the images next to them.

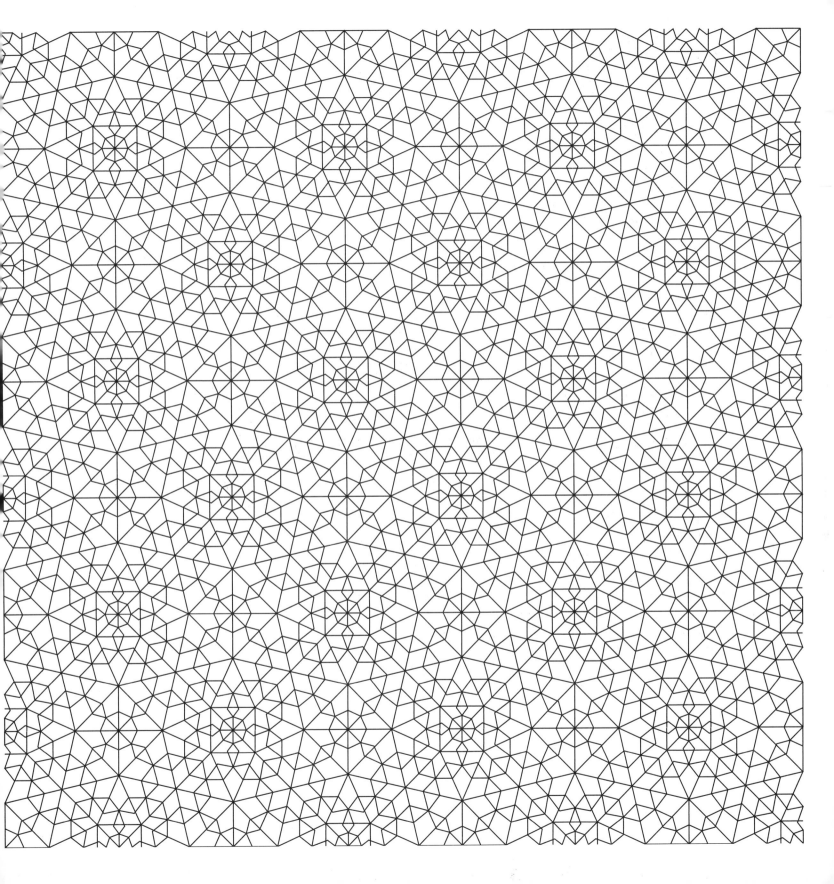

DESIGN # 10

Find the repeating square tiles and build patterns around them.

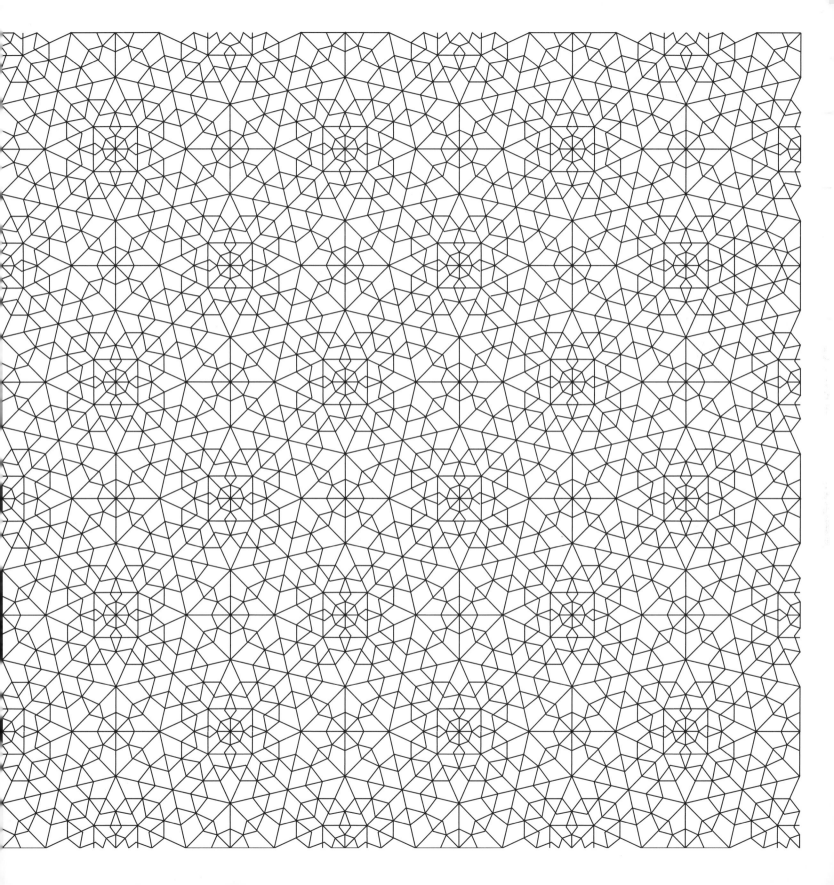

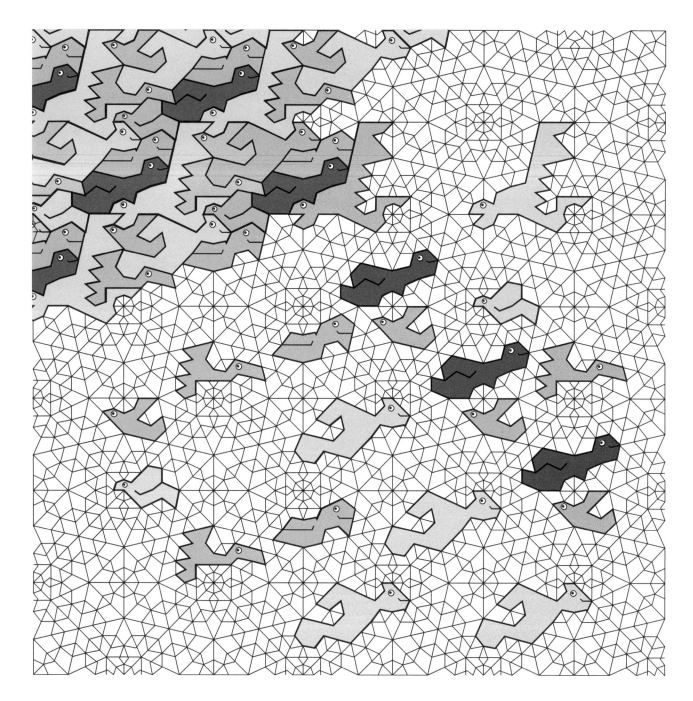

DESIGN # 10

Dragons can fill every gap and repeat to cover the whole design area.

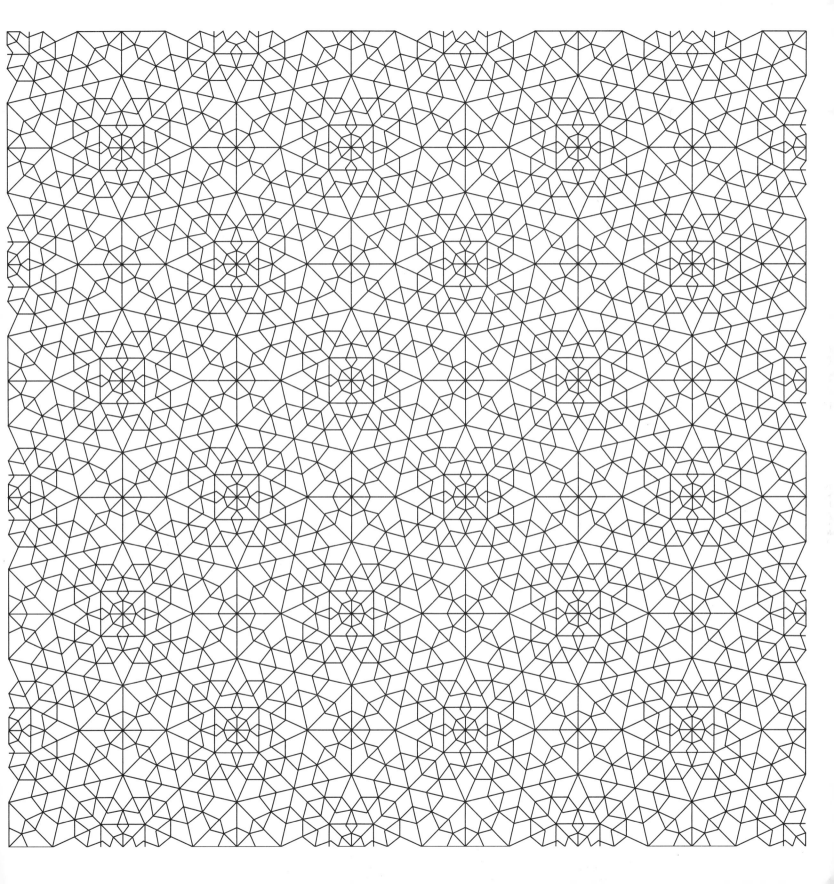

DESIGN # 10

How many birds and dragons can you add to this scene?

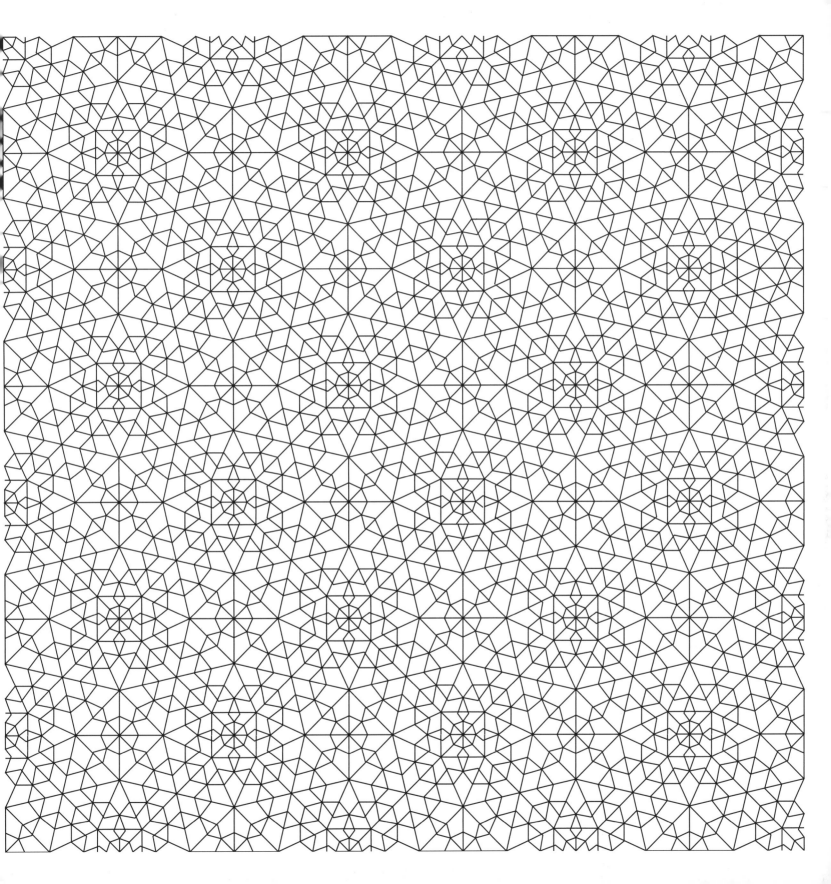

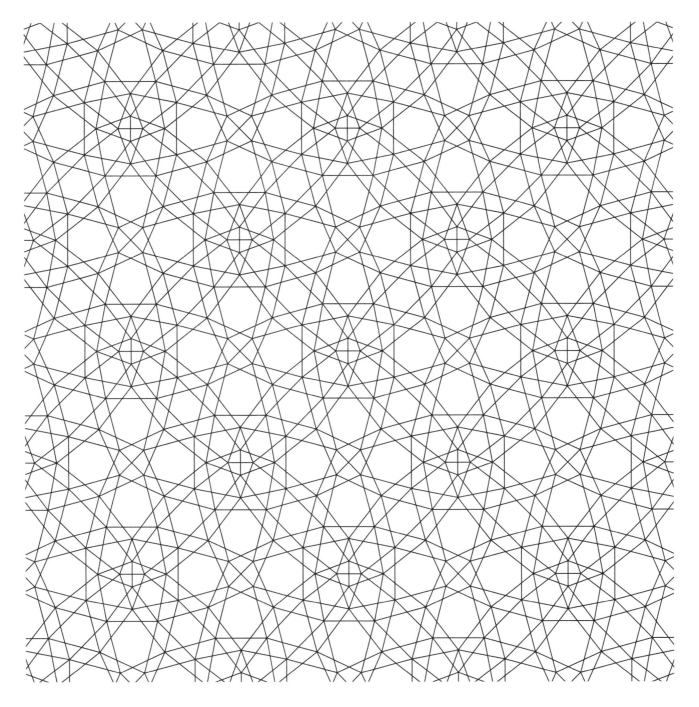

Now that you can find hidden images within a design, it's time to find some on your own. Use your imagination! What images do you see? How many images will you include? What completed scenes will you make?

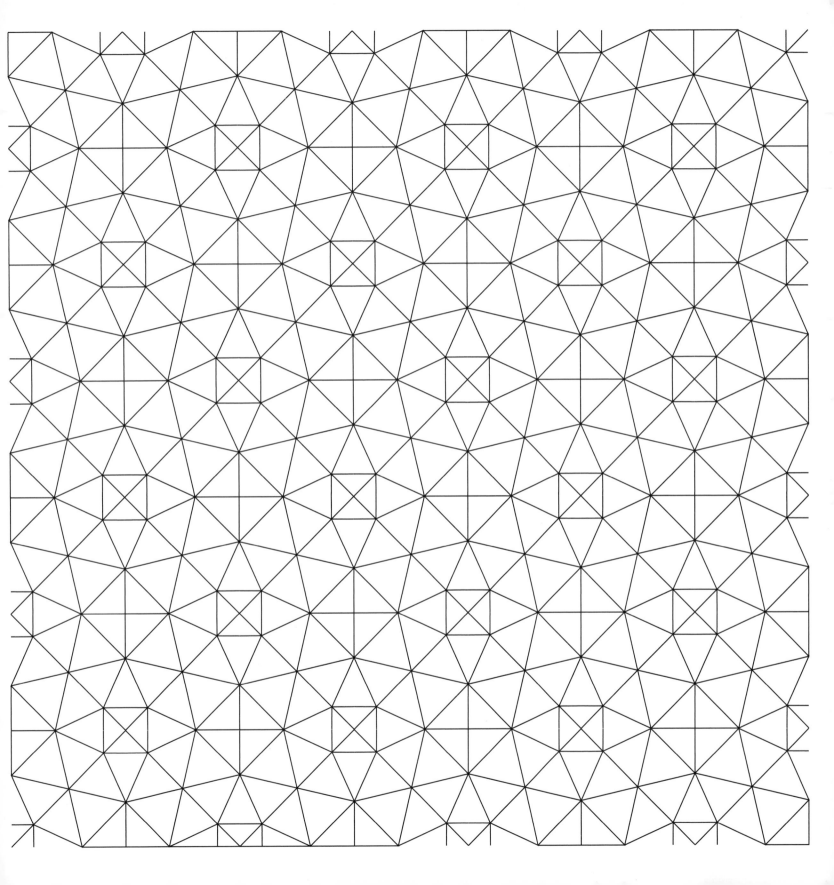

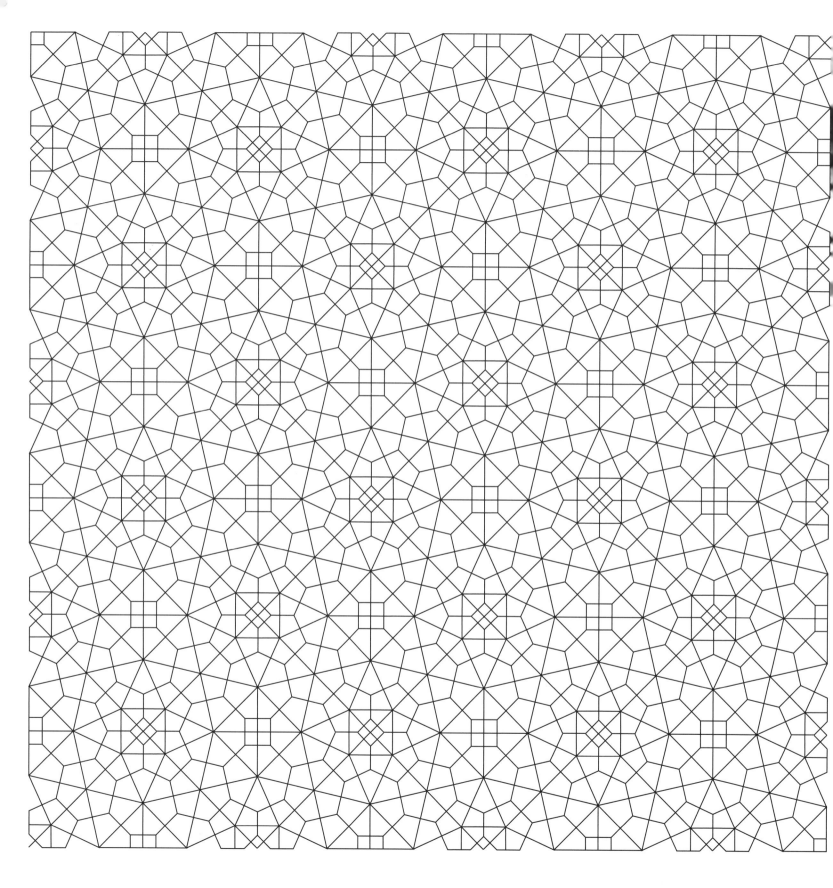

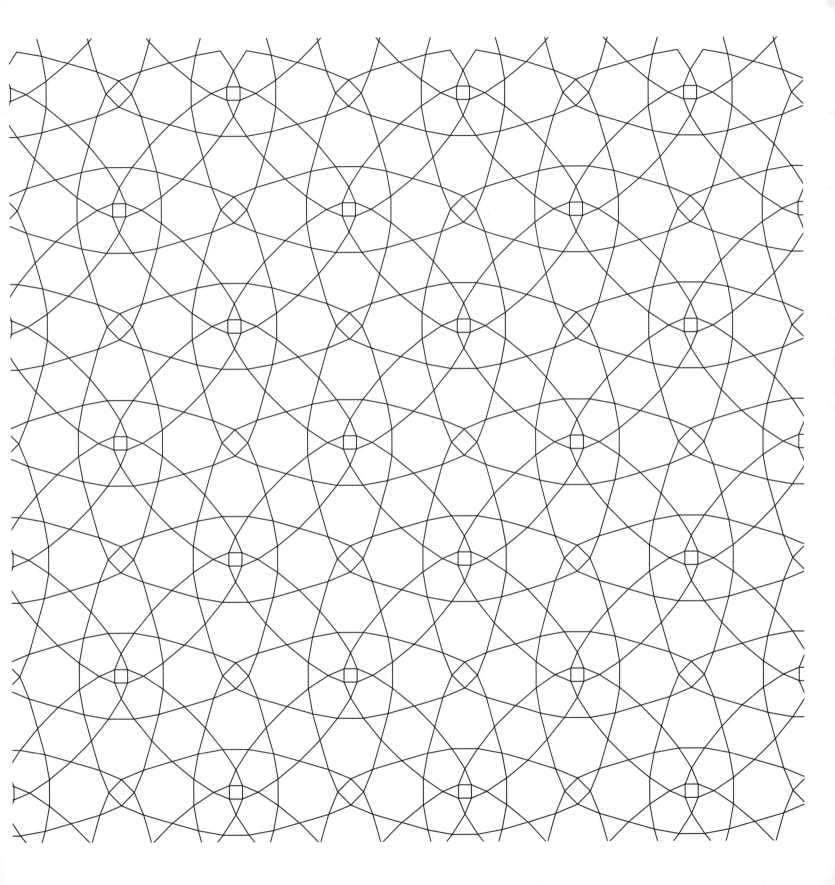

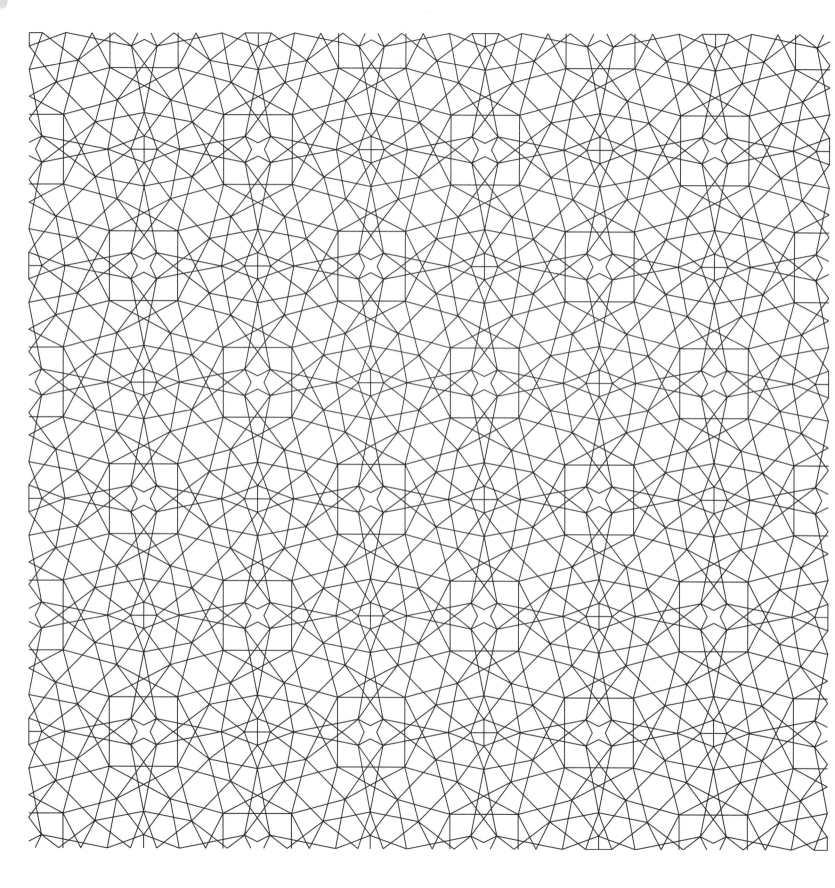

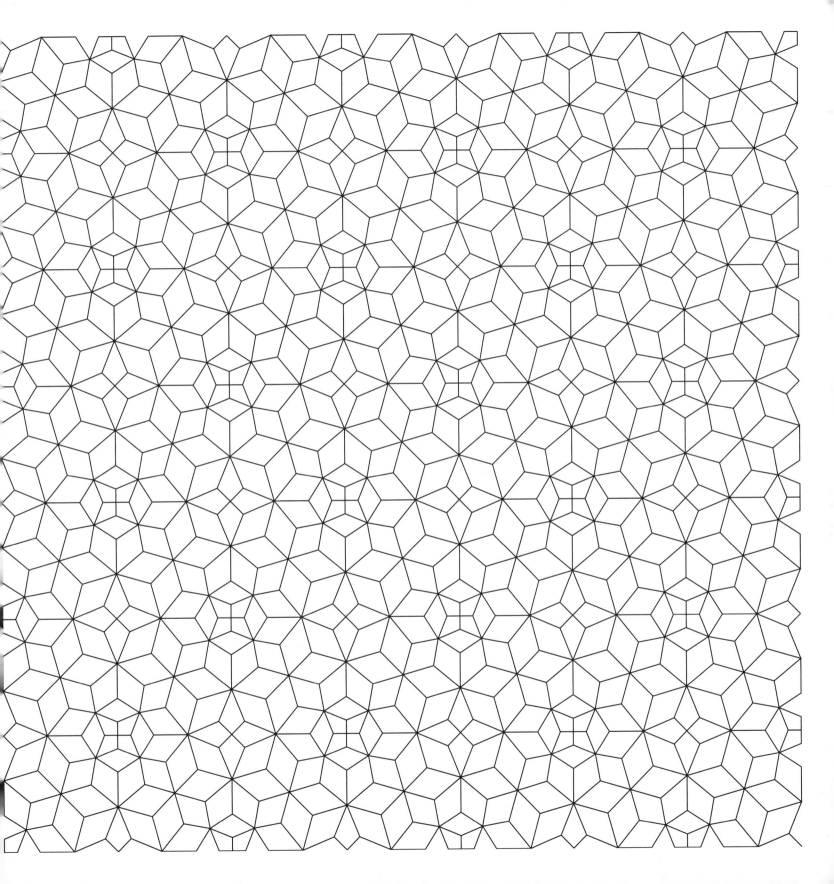

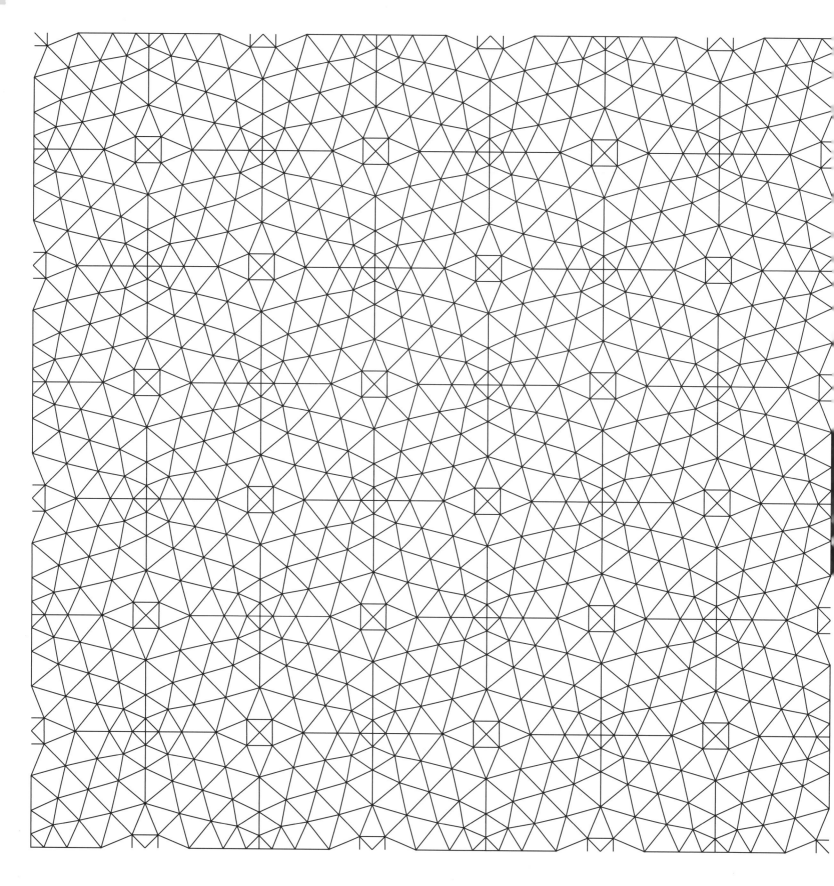

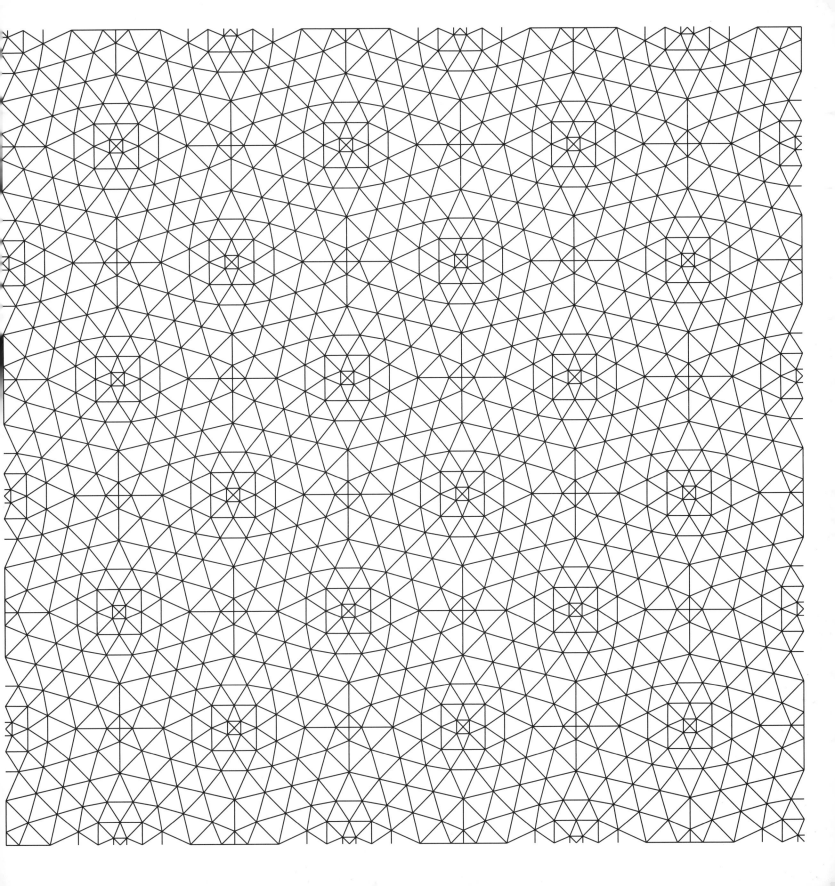

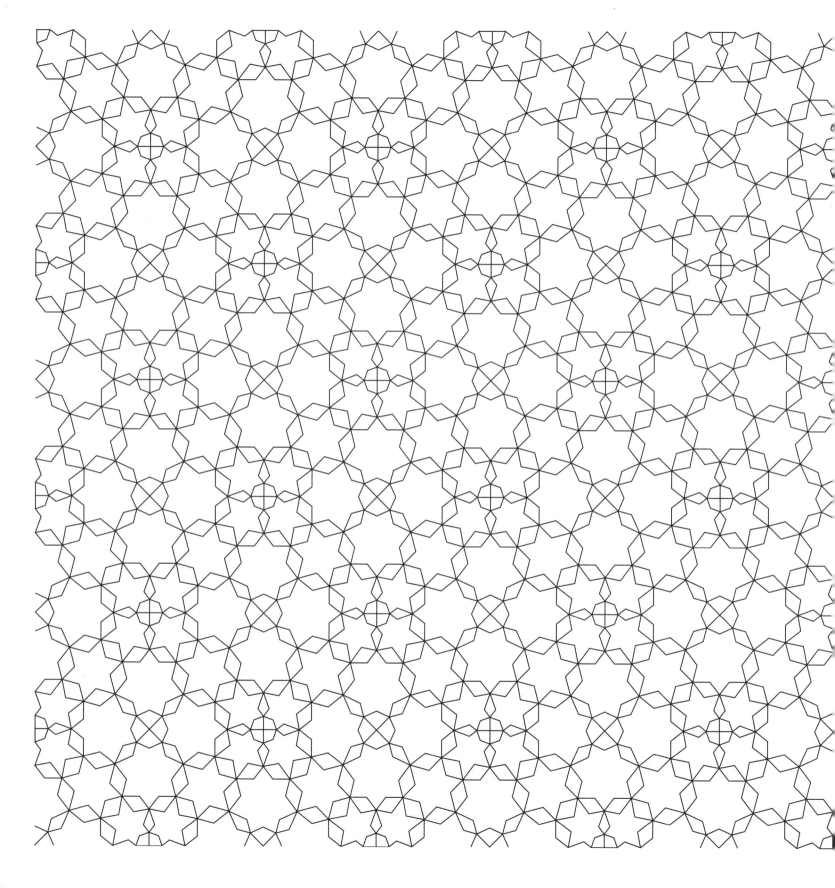

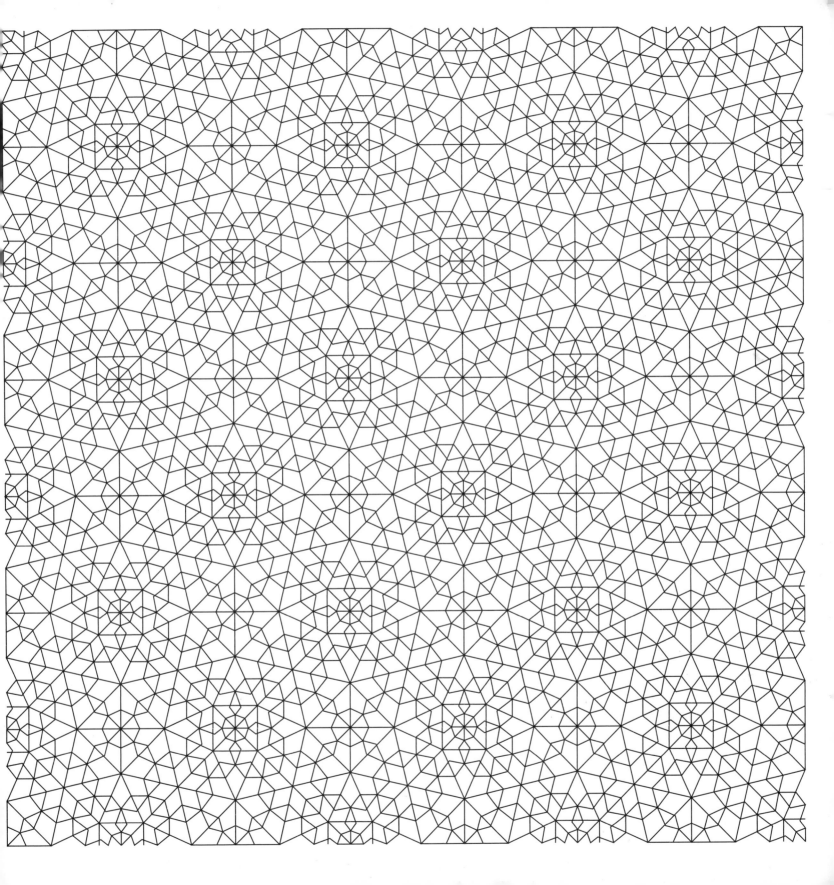

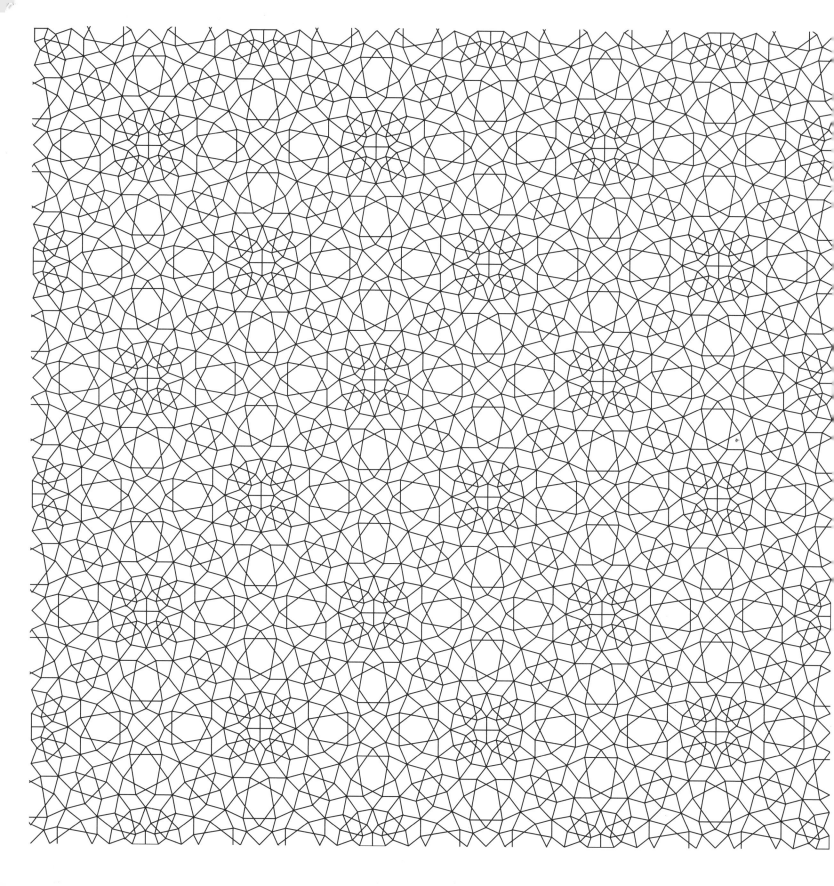